W9-BSH-944

CROCK·POT®
◆ THE ORIGINAL SLOW COOKER ◆

vegetarian
recipes

Publications International, Ltd.

© 2013 Publications International, Ltd.

Text on pages 4 and 5 and recipes on pages 66, 91, 152 and 164 © 2013 Sunbeam Products, Inc. doing business as Jarden Consumer Solutions. All rights reserved. All other recipes © 2013 Publications International, Ltd. Photographs © 2013 Publications International, Ltd. This publication may not be reproduced or quoted in whole or in part by any means whatsoever without written permission from:

Louis Weber, CEO
Publications International, Ltd.
7373 North Cicero Avenue
Lincolnwood, IL 60712

Permission is never granted for commercial purposes.

Crock-Pot® and the Crock-Pot® logo are registered trademarks of Sunbeam Products, Inc. used under license.

Some of the products listed in this publication may be in limited distribution.

Pictured on the front cover: Artichoke Pasta *(page 62)*.

Pictured on the back cover: Vegetarian Chili *(page 94)*.

ISBN-13: 978-1-4508-6490-9
ISBN-10: 1-4508-6490-2

Library of Congress Control Number: 2013930692

Manufactured in China.

8 7 6 5 4 3 2 1

slow cooking hints and tips

To get the most from your **CROCK-POT®** slow cooker, keep the following hints and tips in mind.

Adding Ingredients at the End of the Cooking Time

Certain ingredients are best added toward the end of the cooking time. These include:

- **Milk, sour cream and yogurt:** Add during the last 15 minutes.
- **Fresh herbs:** Fresh herbs such as basil will darken with long cooking, so if you want colorful fresh herbs, add them during the last 15 minutes of cooking or directly to the dish just before serving it.

Pasta and Rice

Converted rice holds up best through slow cooking. If the rice doesn't seem completely cooked after the suggested time, add an extra ½ cup to 1 cup of liquid per cup of rice, and extend the cooking time by 30 to 60 minutes.

Cooking Temperatures and Food Safety

According to the U.S. Department of Agriculture, bacteria in food is killed at a temperature of 165°F. As a result, it's important to follow the recommended cooking times and to keep the cover on your **CROCK-POT®** slow cooker during the cooking process to maintain food-safe temperatures.

Herbs and Spices

When cooking with your **CROCK-POT®** slow cooker, use dried and ground herbs and spices, which work well during long cooking times. However, the flavor and aroma of crushed or ground herbs may differ depending on their shelf life, and their flavor can lessen during the extended cooking time in the **CROCK-POT®** slow cooker.

Cooking for Larger Quantity Yields

Follow these guidelines to make a bigger batch in a larger unit, such as a 5-, 6- or 7-quart **CROCK-POT®** slow cooker:

- Flavorful dried spices such as garlic or chili powder will intensify during long, slow cooking. Add just 25 to 50 percent more spices, as needed, to balance the flavors.
- When preparing a soup or a stew, you may double all ingredients except the liquids, seasonings and dried herbs. Increase liquid volume by half, or adjust as needed.
- To avoid over or undercooking, always fill the stoneware ½ to ¾ full and conform to the recommended cooking times (unless instructed otherwise by our **CROCK-POT®** slow cooker recipes).

• Do not double thickeners such as cornstarch at the beginning. You may always add more thickener later if it's necessary.

Cooking with Frozen Foods

Slow cooking frozen foods requires a longer cooking time than fresh foods because the food needs more time to come up to safe internal temperatures.

Removable Stoneware

The removable stoneware in your **CROCK-POT®** slow cooker makes cleaning easy. However, the stoneware insert can be damaged by sudden changes in temperature. Following are tips on the use and care of your stoneware:

• Don't preheat the **CROCK-POT®** slow cooker.
• Don't place a cold insert into a preheated base.
• Don't place a hot insert on a cold surface or in the refrigerator, and don't fill it with cold water.
• Never place stoneware in the freezer.
• Don't use the stoneware insert if it's cracked; replace it.
• For further safety tips, please refer to the instruction manual that came with your **CROCK-POT®** slow cooker.

international
favorites

cuban black beans and rice

3¾ cups vegetable broth

1½ cups uncooked brown rice

1 onion, chopped

1 jalapeño pepper, seeded and chopped*

3 cloves garlic, minced

2 teaspoons ground cumin

1 teaspoon salt

2 cans (about 15 ounces each) black beans, rinsed and drained

1 tablespoon lime juice

Sour cream and chopped green onions (optional)

Jalapeño peppers can sting and irritate the skin, so wear rubber gloves when handling peppers and do not touch your eyes.

1. Combine broth, rice, onion, jalapeño pepper, garlic, cumin and salt in **CROCK-POT®** slow cooker; mix well. Cover; cook on LOW 7½ hours or until rice is tender.

2. Stir beans and lime juice into **CROCK-POT®** slow cooker. Cover; cook on LOW 15 to 20 minutes or until heated through. Garnish with sour cream and green onions.

Makes 4 to 6 servings

asian sweet potato and corn stew

1 tablespoon vegetable oil

1 large onion, chopped

2 tablespoons minced fresh ginger

½ jalapeño or serrano pepper, seeded and minced*

2 cloves garlic, minced

1 cup corn

2 teaspoons curry powder

1 can (about 14 ounces) unsweetened coconut milk, well shaken

1 teaspoon cornstarch

1 can (about 14 ounces) vegetable broth

1 tablespoon soy sauce

4 sweet potatoes, peeled and cut into ¾-inch cubes

Hot cooked jasmine or long grain rice

Chopped fresh cilantro (optional)

*Jalapeño and serrano peppers can sting and irritate the skin, so wear rubber gloves when handling peppers and do not touch your eyes.

1. Heat oil in large skillet over medium heat. Add onion, ginger, jalapeño pepper and garlic; cook and stir about 5 minutes or until onion softens. Remove from heat; stir in corn and curry powder.

2. Stir coconut milk into cornstarch in **CROCK-POT®** slow cooker until smooth. Stir in broth and soy sauce. Carefully add sweet potatoes; top with corn mixture. Cover; cook on LOW 5 to 6 hours or until sweet potatoes are tender. Stir gently to smooth cooking liquid (coconut milk may look curdled) without breaking up sweet potatoes. Adjust seasoning to taste with additional soy sauce. Spoon over rice in serving bowls and sprinkle with cilantro, if desired.

Makes 6 servings

Serving Suggestion
Garnish with coarsely chopped dry-roasted peanuts and chopped green onions for extra flavor and crunch.

mushroom and vegetable ragoût over polenta

Ragoût

- **3 tablespoons extra virgin olive oil**
- **8 ounces sliced white or brown mushrooms**
- **8 ounces shiitake mushrooms, stemmed and thinly sliced**
- **½ cup Madeira wine**
- **1 can (28 ounces) crushed tomatoes**
- **1 can (about 15 ounces) chickpeas, rinsed and drained**
- **1 medium onion, chopped**
- **1 can (6 ounces) tomato paste**
- **4 cloves garlic, minced**
- **1 sprig fresh rosemary**

Polenta

- **2 cups water**
- **2 cups whole milk**
- **¼ teaspoon salt**
- **2 cups uncooked instant polenta**
- **½ cup grated Parmesan cheese**

1. Heat oil in large skillet over medium-high heat. Add mushrooms; cook and stir 8 to 10 minutes or until browned. Add wine; cook 1 minute or until liquid is reduced by half. Transfer to **CROCK-POT®** slow cooker.

2. Stir tomatoes, chickpeas, onion, tomato paste, garlic and rosemary into **CROCK-POT®** slow cooker. Cover; cook on LOW 6 hours or until vegetables are tender. Remove and discard rosemary.

3. For polenta, combine water, milk and salt in large saucepan; bring to a boil over medium-high heat. Slowly whisk in polenta in steady stream. Cook 4 to 5 minutes, whisking constantly, until thick and creamy.

4. Remove polenta from heat; stir in cheese. Serve with ragoût.

Makes 6 servings

asiago and asparagus risotto-style rice

2 **cups chopped onions**

1 **can (about 14 ounces) vegetable broth**

1 **cup uncooked converted rice**

2 **cloves garlic, minced**

½ **pound asparagus spears, trimmed and cut into 1-inch pieces**

¾ **cup half-and-half, divided**

½ **cup grated Asiago cheese, plus additional for garnish**

¼ **cup (½ stick) butter, cubed**

2 **ounces pine nuts or slivered almonds, toasted***

1 **teaspoon salt**

*To toast pine nuts, spread in single layer in heavy skillet. Cook over medium heat 1 to 2 minutes or until nuts are lightly browned, stirring frequently.

1. Combine onions, broth, rice and garlic in **CROCK-POT®** slow cooker; mix well. Cover; cook on HIGH 2 hours or until rice is tender.

2. Stir in asparagus and ½ cup half-and-half. Cover; cook on HIGH 20 minutes or until asparagus is crisp-tender.

3. Turn off heat. Stir in remaining ¼ cup half-and-half, ½ cup cheese, butter, pine nuts and salt; let stand , covered, 5 minutes to allow cheese to melt slightly. Fluff with fork. Garnish with additional cheese.

Makes 4 servings

Tip

Risotto is a classic creamy rice dish from northern Italy. It can be made with a wide variety of ingredients; fresh vegetables and flavorful cheeses such as Asiago work especially well in risottos. Parmesan cheese, white wine and herbs are also popular additions.

open-face provençal vegetable sandwich

2 cups sliced shiitake mushroom caps

1 large zucchini, halved lengthwise and cut into ¼-inch slices

1 red bell pepper, quartered lengthwise and thinly sliced

1 small onion, cut into ¼-inch slices

¼ cup vegetable broth

¼ cup pitted kalamata olives

1 jalapeño pepper, seeded and minced*

2 tablespoons capers

1½ tablespoons olive oil, divided

1 clove garlic, minced

½ teaspoon dried oregano

¼ teaspoon salt

¼ teaspoon black pepper

4 teaspoons white wine vinegar

Crusty bread, cut into thick slices

¾ cup (3 ounces) shredded mozzarella cheese (optional)

*Jalapeño peppers can sting and irritate the skin, so wear rubber gloves when handling peppers and do not touch your eyes.

1. Combine mushrooms, zucchini, bell pepper, onion, broth, olives, jalapeño pepper, capers, 1 tablespoon oil, garlic, oregano, salt and black pepper in **CROCK-POT®** slow cooker. Cover; cook on LOW 5 to 6 hours.

2. Turn off heat. Stir in vinegar and remaining ½ tablespoon oil. Let stand, uncovered, 15 to 30 minutes or until vegetables absorb some of liquid. Season with additional salt and black pepper, if desired.

3. Spoon vegetables onto bread. If desired, sprinkle each serving with 2 tablespoons mozzarella cheese and broil 30 seconds or until cheese melts and browns.

Makes 6 servings

black bean and mushroom chilaquiles

2 tablespoons olive oil

1 medium onion, chopped

1 medium green bell pepper, chopped

1 jalapeño or serrano pepper, seeded and minced*

2 cans (about 15 ounces each) black beans, rinsed and drained

1 can (about 14 ounces) diced tomatoes

10 ounces white mushrooms, cut into quarters

1½ teaspoons ground cumin

1½ teaspoons dried oregano

1 cup (4 ounces) shredded sharp white Cheddar cheese, plus additional for garnish

6 cups baked tortilla chips, coarsely crushed

*Jalapeño and serrano peppers can sting and irritate the skin, so wear rubber gloves when handling peppers and do not touch your eyes.

1. Heat oil in medium skillet over medium heat. Add onion, bell pepper and jalapeño pepper; cook and stir about 5 minutes or until onion softens, stirring occasionally. Transfer to **CROCK-POT®** slow cooker. Add beans, tomatoes, mushrooms, cumin and oregano. Cover; cook on LOW 6 hours or on HIGH 3 hours.

2. Turn off heat. Sprinkle 1 cup Cheddar cheese over beans and mushrooms; let stand, covered, 5 minutes or until cheese is melted. Stir to combine melted cheese.

3. Place tortilla chips in serving bowls. Top with black bean mixture and sprinkle with additional cheese, if desired.

Makes 6 servings

vegetable jollof rice

1 medium eggplant (about 1¼ pounds), cut into 1-inch cubes

1¾ teaspoons salt, divided

3 tablespoons vegetable oil, divided

1 medium onion, chopped

1 green bell pepper, chopped

3 carrots, cut into ½-inch-thick slices

2 cloves garlic, minced

1½ cups uncooked converted rice

1 tablespoon plus ½ teaspoon chili powder

1 can (28 ounces) diced tomatoes

1 can (about 14 ounces) vegetable broth

1. Place eggplant cubes in colander. Sprinkle with 1 teaspoon salt; toss to coat. Let stand in sink 1 hour to drain. Rinse under cold water; drain. Pat dry with paper towels.

2. Heat 1 tablespoon oil in large skillet over medium-high heat. Cook half of eggplant, turning to brown on all sides. Remove eggplant to plate as it is browned. Repeat with remaining eggplant and 1 tablespoon oil.

3. Wipe out skillet with paper towels. Heat remaining 1 tablespoon oil in skillet over medium-high heat. Add onion, bell pepper, carrots and garlic; cook and stir until onion is soft but not browned. Transfer to **CROCK-POT®** slow cooker. Stir in rice, chili powder and remaining ¾ teaspoon salt; mix well.

4. Drain tomatoes over 4-cup measuring cup. Add broth to juice and enough water to measure 4 cups. Pour into **CROCK-POT®** slow cooker. Add drained tomatoes; stir to level rice. Top with eggplant. Cover; cook on LOW 3½ to 4 hours or until rice is tender and liquid is absorbed. Stir well before serving.

Makes 6 servings

Tip
Jollof Rice (also spelled "jolof" or sometimes "djolof") is an important dish in West African cuisine.

pasta fagioli soup

2 cans (about 14 ounces each) vegetable broth

1 can (about 15 ounces) Great Northern beans, rinsed and drained

1 can (about 14 ounces) diced tomatoes

2 zucchini, quartered lengthwise and sliced

1 tablespoon olive oil

1½ teaspoons minced garlic

½ teaspoon dried basil

½ teaspoon dried oregano

½ cup uncooked ditalini, tubetti or small shell pasta

½ cup garlic seasoned croutons

½ cup grated Asiago or Romano cheese

3 tablespoons chopped fresh basil or Italian parsley (optional)

1. Combine broth, beans, tomatoes, zucchini, oil, garlic, dried basil and oregano in **CROCK-POT®** slow cooker; mix well. Cover; cook on LOW 3 to 4 hours.

2. Stir in pasta. Cover; cook on LOW 1 hour or until pasta is tender.

3. Serve soup with croutons and cheese. Garnish with fresh basil.

Makes 5 to 6 servings

Tip
Only small pasta varieties like ditalini or tubetti pasta should be used in this recipe. The low heat of a **CROCK-POT®** slow cooker will not allow larger pasta shapes to cook completely.

greek lemon and rice soup

3 cans (about 14 ounces each) vegetable broth

½ cup uncooked long grain white rice

3 egg yolks

¼ cup fresh lemon juice

¼ teaspoon salt

⅛ teaspoon ground white pepper*

4 thin lemon slices (optional)

4 teaspoons finely chopped fresh parsley (optional)

*Or substitute ground black pepper.

1. Combine broth and rice in **CROCK-POT®** slow cooker; mix well. Cover; cook on HIGH 2 to 3 hours or until rice is tender.

2. Whisk egg yolks and lemon juice in medium bowl. Whisk large spoonful of hot rice mixture into egg yolk mixture. Whisk egg yolk mixture back into **CROCK-POT®** slow cooker.

3. Turn **CROCK-POT®** slow cooker to LOW. Cover; cook on LOW 10 minutes. Season with salt and pepper. Ladle soup into serving bowls; garnish with lemon slices and parsley.

Makes 4 servings

saag paneer

- **2 onions, finely chopped**
- **8 cloves garlic, minced**
- **1 teaspoon ground coriander**
- **1 teaspoon ground cumin**
- **½ teaspoon pumpkin pie spice**
- **½ teaspoon cardamom**
- **½ teaspoon salt**
- **2 packages (10 ounces each) frozen chopped spinach, thawed and squeezed dry**
- **2 packages (9 ounces each) frozen chopped creamed spinach, thawed**
- **2 tablespoons butter**
- **8 ounces paneer, cut into ½-inch cubes***

*Paneer is a firm fresh cheese used in South Asian cuisines. Substitute any firm white cheese or extra firm tofu.

1. Combine onions, garlic, coriander, cumin, pumpkin pie spice, cardamom and salt in **CROCK-POT®** slow cooker. Add spinach, creamed spinach and butter; mix well. Cover; cook on LOW 4½ to 5 hours or until onions are soft.

2. Add paneer; cover and cook on LOW 30 minutes or until paneer is heated through.

Makes 10 servings

chickpea and vegetable curry

1 can (about 14 ounces) unsweetened coconut milk

1 cup vegetable broth, divided

2 teaspoons curry powder

¼ teaspoon ground red pepper

2 cups cut fresh green beans (1-inch pieces)

1 can (about 15 ounces) chickpeas, rinsed and drained

2 carrots, very thinly sliced

½ cup golden raisins

¼ cup all-purpose flour

2 cups hot cooked couscous

Chopped green onion and toasted sliced almonds (optional)

1. Coat inside of **CROCK-POT®** slow cooker with nonstick cooking spray. Combine coconut milk, ¾ cup broth, curry powder and ground red pepper in **CROCK-POT®** slow cooker. Stir in green beans, chickpeas, carrots and raisins; mix well. Cover; cook on LOW 6 to 7 hours or on HIGH 2½ to 3 hours or until vegetables are tender.

2. Whisk remaining ¼ cup broth into flour in small bowl until smooth; stir into vegetable mixture. Turn **CROCK-POT®** slow cooker to HIGH. Cover; cook on HIGH 15 minutes or until thickened. Ladle into shallow bowls; top with couscous. Sprinkle with green onion and almonds, if desired.

Makes 4 servings

ratatouille

1 tablespoon olive oil

1 baby eggplant, diced *or* 1 cup diced regular eggplant

2 medium tomatoes, chopped

1 small zucchini, diced

1 cup sliced mushrooms

½ cup tomato purée

1 large shallot *or* ½ small onion, chopped

1 clove garlic, minced

¾ teaspoon dried oregano

⅛ teaspoon dried rosemary

⅛ teaspoon black pepper

2 tablespoons shredded fresh basil

2 teaspoons lemon juice

½ teaspoon salt

¼ cup shredded Parmesan cheese

1. Heat oil in large skillet over medium-high heat. Add eggplant; cook and stir about 5 minutes or until lightly browned. Transfer to **CROCK-POT®** slow cooker.

2. Add tomatoes, zucchini, mushrooms, tomato purée, shallot, garlic, oregano, rosemary and pepper. Cover; cook on LOW 6 hours.

3. Stir in basil, lemon juice and salt. Turn off heat; let stand 5 minutes. Serve with cheese.

Makes 4 servings

jamaican quinoa and sweet potato stew

3 cups vegetable broth

1 large or 2 small sweet potatoes (12 ounces), cut into ¾-inch pieces

1 cup uncooked quinoa, rinsed and drained

1 red bell pepper, cut into ¾-inch pieces

1 tablespoon jerk seasoning

¼ cup chopped fresh cilantro

¼ cup sliced almonds, toasted*

Hot pepper sauce (optional)

*To toast almonds, spread in single layer in heavy skillet. Cook over medium heat 1 to 2 minutes or until nuts are lightly browned, stirring frequently.

1. Coat inside of **CROCK-POT®** slow cooker with nonstick cooking spray. Combine broth, sweet potato, quinoa, bell pepper and jerk seasoning in **CROCK-POT®** slow cooker. Cover; cook on LOW 5 to 6 hours or on HIGH 2 to 2½ hours or until vegetables are tender.

2. Ladle into bowls; top with cilantro and almonds. Serve with hot pepper sauce, if desired.

Makes 4 servings

channa chat (indian-spiced snack mix)

2 teaspoons canola oil

1 medium onion, finely chopped, divided

2 cloves garlic, minced

2 cans (about 15 ounces each) chickpeas, rinsed and drained

¼ cup vegetable broth or water

2 teaspoons tomato paste

¼ teaspoon ground cinnamon

¼ teaspoon ground cumin

¼ teaspoon black pepper

1 whole bay leaf

½ cup balsamic vinegar

1 tablespoon packed brown sugar

1 plum tomato, chopped

½ jalapeño pepper, seeded and minced *or* ¼ teaspoon ground red pepper (optional)*

½ cup crisp rice cereal

3 tablespoons chopped fresh cilantro (optional)

Jalapeño peppers can sting and irritate the skin, so wear rubber gloves when handling peppers and do not touch your eyes.

1. Heat oil in small skillet over medium-high heat. Add half of onion and garlic. Reduce heat to medium; cook and stir 2 minutes or until soft. Transfer to **CROCK-POT®** slow cooker. Stir in chickpeas, broth, tomato paste, cinnamon, cumin, black pepper and bay leaf. Cover; cook on LOW 6 hours or on HIGH 3 hours. Remove and discard bay leaf.

2. Remove chickpeas to large bowl with slotted spoon. Cool 15 minutes. Meanwhile, combine vinegar and brown sugar in small saucepan; cook over medium-low heat until vinegar is reduced by half and mixture becomes syrupy, stirring frequently.

3. Add tomato, remaining onion and jalapeño pepper, if desired, to chickpeas; toss to combine. Gently fold in cereal. Drizzle with balsamic syrup and garnish with cilantro.

Makes 6 to 8 servings

southwestern stuffed peppers

4 green bell peppers

1 can (about 15 ounces) black beans, rinsed and drained

1 cup (4 ounces) shredded pepper jack cheese

¾ cup medium salsa

½ cup frozen corn

½ cup chopped green onions

⅓ cup uncooked long grain white rice

1 teaspoon chili powder

½ teaspoon ground cumin

Sour cream (optional)

1. Cut thin slice off top of each bell pepper. Carefully remove seeds and membrane, leaving pepper whole.

2. Combine beans, cheese, salsa, corn, green onions, rice, chili powder and cumin in medium bowl. Spoon filling evenly into peppers. Place peppers in **CROCK-POT®** slow cooker.

3. Cover; cook on LOW 4 to 6 hours. Serve with sour cream, if desired.

Makes 4 servings

Tip
For firmer rice in the finished dish, substitute converted rice for regular long grain white rice.

italian escarole and white bean stew

1 **tablespoon olive oil**

1 **medium onion, chopped**

3 **medium carrots, cut into ½-inch-thick rounds**

2 **cloves garlic, minced**

1 **can (about 14 ounces) vegetable broth**

1 **head escarole (about 12 ounces)**

¼ **teaspoon red pepper flakes**

2 **cans (about 15 ounces each) Great Northern beans, rinsed and drained**

Salt

Grated Parmesan cheese (optional)

1. Heat oil in medium skillet over medium-high heat. Add onion and carrots; cook and stir about 5 minutes or until onion softens. Add garlic; cook and stir about 1 minute or until fragrant. Transfer to **CROCK-POT®** slow cooker. Pour in broth.

2. Trim off base of escarole. Cut crosswise into 1-inch strips. Wash well in large bowl of cold water. Lift out by handfuls, leaving sand or dirt in bottom of bowl. Shake to remove excess water, but do not dry. Add to vegetable mixture in **CROCK-POT®** slow cooker. Sprinkle with red pepper flakes. Top with beans.

3. Cover; cook on LOW 7 to 8 hours or on HIGH 3½ to 4 hours or until escarole is wilted and very tender. Season with salt. Serve with cheese, if desired.

Makes 4 servings

Tip

Escarole is very leafy and easily fills a 4½-quart **CROCK-POT®** slow cooker when raw, but shrinks dramatically as it cooks down. This recipe makes 4 servings, but can easily be doubled. Simply double all of the ingredients and use a 6-quart **CROCK-POT®** slow cooker.

eggplant parmesan

¼ **cup all-purpose flour**

1 **teaspoon dried oregano**

1 **teaspoon dried basil**

½ **teaspoon salt**

1 **egg**

2 **teaspoons cold water**

1 **large eggplant (about 1 pound), ends trimmed, peeled and cut crosswise into 8 slices**

2 **tablespoons extra virgin olive oil, divided**

2¼ **cups spicy marinara sauce**

½ **cup panko bread crumbs**

1½ **cups (6 ounces) shredded Italian cheese blend or mozzarella cheese, divided**

Chopped fresh basil (optional)

1. Combine flour, oregano, dried basil and salt in shallow dish or pie plate. Beat egg and water in another shallow dish or pie plate.

2. Dip each slice of eggplant in egg mixture, letting excess drip back into dish. Dredge in flour mixture, coating both sides lightly. Heat 1 tablespoon oil in large nonstick skillet over medium heat. Add 4 eggplant slices to skillet; cook 3 to 4 minutes per side or until lightly browned. Repeat with remaining oil and 4 eggplant slices.

3. Coat inside of **CROCK-POT®** slow cooker with nonstick cooking spray. Spread ¾ cup marinara sauce in bottom of **CROCK-POT®** slow cooker. Arrange 4 eggplant slices over sauce, overlapping if necessary. Top with ¼ cup bread crumbs and ½ cup cheese. Layer with ¾ cup marinara sauce, 4 eggplant slices, ¼ cup bread crumbs and ½ cup cheese. Spoon remaining marinara sauce over cheese. Cover; cook on LOW 4 to 5 hours or on HIGH 2 to 2½ hours.

4. Turn off heat. Sprinkle with remaining ½ cup cheese; let stand, covered, 5 minutes or until cheese melts. Garnish with fresh basil.

Makes 4 servings

mediterranean frittata

Butter, softened

- 3 **tablespoons extra virgin olive oil**
- 1 **large onion, chopped**
- 8 **ounces (about 2 cups) sliced mushrooms**
- 6 **cloves garlic, sliced**
- 1 **teaspoon dried basil**
- 1 **medium red bell pepper, chopped**
- 1 **package (10 ounces) frozen chopped spinach, thawed and squeezed dry**
- ¼ **cup sliced kalamata olives**
- 8 **eggs, beaten**
- 4 **ounces feta cheese, crumbled**
- ½ **teaspoon salt**
- ¼ **teaspoon black pepper**

1. Grease inside bottom and lower third of 5- to 6-quart **CROCK-POT®** slow cooker with butter. Heat oil in large skillet over medium-high heat. Add onion, mushrooms, garlic and basil; cook and stir 2 to 3 minutes or until vegetables are slightly softened. Add bell pepper; cook and stir 4 to 5 minutes or until vegetables are tender. Stir in spinach; cook 2 minutes. Stir in olives. Transfer to **CROCK-POT®** slow cooker.

2. Whisk eggs, cheese, salt and black pepper in large bowl. Pour over vegetables in **CROCK-POT®** slow cooker. Cover; cook on LOW 2½ to 3 hours or on HIGH 1¼ to 1½ hours or until eggs are set. Cut into wedges.

Makes 4 to 6 servings

mexican rice, bean and cheese burritos

1 cup uncooked converted rice

1 can (about 15 ounces) black beans, rinsed and drained

1 can (about 14 ounces) fire-roasted diced tomatoes

1 medium onion, chopped

3 cloves garlic, minced

1 jalapeño pepper, chopped*

2 teaspoons chili powder

1 cup ricotta cheese

½ cup water

2 cups (8 ounces) shredded Monterey Jack cheese

3 tablespoons chopped fresh cilantro

6 flour tortillas (10 inches)

¾ cup prepared black bean and corn salsa

Jalapeño peppers can sting and irritate the skin, so wear rubber gloves when handling peppers and do not touch your eyes.

1. Coat inside of **CROCK-POT®** slow cooker with nonstick cooking spray. Add rice, beans, tomatoes, onion, garlic, jalapeño pepper, chili powder, ricotta cheese and water to **CROCK-POT®** slow cooker. Cover; cook on LOW 4 hours or until rice is tender.

2. Stir in Monterey Jack cheese and cilantro. Warm tortillas according to package directions. Place 1 cup filling on each tortilla and roll up. Serve with salsa.

Makes 6 servings

curried potatoes, cauliflower and peas

1 tablespoon vegetable oil

1 onion, chopped

2 tablespoons minced fresh ginger

2 cloves garlic, chopped

2 pounds unpeeled red potatoes, cut into ½-inch-thick slices

1 teaspoon garam masala*

1 teaspoon salt

1 small head cauliflower (about 1¼ pounds), trimmed and broken into florets

1 cup vegetable broth or water

2 ripe plum tomatoes, seeded and chopped

1 cup peas

Hot cooked basmati or long grain rice

*Garam masala is a blend of Indian spices available in the spice aisle of many supermarkets. If garam masala is unavailable substitute ½ teaspoon ground cumin and ½ teaspoon ground coriander seeds.

1. Heat oil in large skillet over medium heat. Add onion, ginger and garlic; cook and stir about 5 minutes or until onion softens. Remove from heat.

2. Place potatoes in **CROCK-POT®** slow cooker. Mix garam masala and salt in small bowl. Sprinkle half of spice mixture over potatoes. Top with onion mixture, then cauliflower. Sprinkle with remaining spice mixture. Pour in broth. Cover; cook on HIGH 3½ hours.

3. Gently stir in tomatoes and peas. Cover; cook on HIGH 30 minutes or until potatoes are tender. Stir gently. Serve over rice.

Makes 6 servings

vegetarian paella

2 teaspoons canola oil

1 cup chopped onion

2 cloves garlic, minced

2¼ cups vegetable broth

1 can (about 14 ounces) stewed tomatoes

1 small zucchini, halved lengthwise and cut into ½-inch slices (about 1¼ cups)

1 cup uncooked brown rice

1 cup coarsely chopped carrots

1 cup chopped red bell pepper

1 teaspoon Italian seasoning

½ teaspoon ground turmeric

⅛ teaspoon ground red pepper

1 can (14 ounces) quartered artichoke hearts, drained

½ cup frozen baby peas

¾ teaspoon salt

1. Heat oil in large nonstick skillet over medium-high heat. Add onion; cook and stir 6 to 7 minutes or until tender. Stir in garlic. Transfer to **CROCK-POT®** slow cooker.

2. Add broth, tomatoes, zucchini, rice, carrots, bell pepper, Italian seasoning, turmeric and ground red pepper to **CROCK-POT®** slow cooker; mix well. Cover; cook on LOW 4 hours or on HIGH 2 hours or until liquid is absorbed.

3. Stir in artichokes and peas. Season with salt. Cover; cook on LOW 5 to 10 minutes or until vegetables are tender.

Makes 6 servings

curried vegetable and cashew stew

2 medium potatoes, cut into ½-inch cubes

1 can (about 15 ounces) chickpeas, rinsed and drained

1 can (about 14 ounces) petite diced tomatoes

1 large eggplant (about 1 pound), cut into ½-inch cubes

1 medium onion, chopped

1 cup vegetable broth

2 tablespoons quick-cooking tapioca

2 teaspoons grated fresh ginger

2 teaspoons curry powder

½ teaspoon salt

¼ teaspoon black pepper

1 medium zucchini (about 8 ounces), cut into ½-inch cubes

1 cup golden raisins

½ cup frozen peas

½ cup lightly salted cashews

1. Combine potatoes, chickpeas, tomatoes, eggplant, onion, broth, tapioca, ginger, curry powder, salt and pepper in **CROCK-POT®** slow cooker. Cover; cook on LOW 8 to 9 hours.

2. Stir zucchini, raisins, peas and cashews into **CROCK-POT®** slow cooker. Turn **CROCK-POT®** slow cooker to HIGH. Cover; cook on HIGH 1 hour or until zucchini is tender.

Makes 6 servings

risi bisi

1½ **cups uncooked converted long grain rice**

¾ **cup chopped onion**

2 **cloves garlic, minced**

2 **cans (about 14 ounces each) vegetable broth**

⅓ **cup water**

¾ **teaspoon Italian seasoning**

½ **teaspoon dried basil**

½ **cup frozen peas**

¼ **cup grated Parmesan cheese**

¼ **cup toasted pine nuts (optional)***

To toast pine nuts, spread in single layer in heavy skillet. Cook over medium heat 1 to 2 minutes or until nuts are lightly browned, stirring frequently.

1. Combine rice, onion and garlic in **CROCK-POT®** slow cooker.

2. Bring broth and water to a boil in medium saucepan. Stir broth mixture, Italian seasoning and basil into rice mixture in **CROCK-POT®** slow cooker; mix well. Cover; cook on LOW 2 to 3 hours or until liquid is absorbed.

3. Add peas to **CROCK-POT®** slow cooker. Cover; cook on LOW 1 hour. Stir in cheese. Sprinkle with pine nuts, if desired.

Makes 6 servings

minestrone alla milanese

2 cans (about 14 ounces each) vegetable broth

1 can (about 14 ounces) diced tomatoes

1 cup diced red potatoes

1 cup coarsely chopped carrots

1 cup coarsely chopped green cabbage

1 cup sliced zucchini

¾ cup chopped onion

¾ cup sliced fresh green beans

¾ cup coarsely chopped celery

¾ cup water

2 tablespoons olive oil

1 clove garlic, minced

½ teaspoon dried basil

¼ teaspoon dried rosemary

1 whole bay leaf

1 can (about 15 ounces) cannellini beans, rinsed and drained

Shredded Parmesan cheese (optional)

1. Combine all ingredients except cannellini beans and cheese in **CROCK-POT®** slow cooker; mix well. Cover; cook on LOW 5 to 6 hours.

2. Add cannellini beans. Cover; cook on LOW 1 hour or until vegetables are tender.

3. Remove and discard bay leaf. Serve with cheese, if desired.

Makes 8 to 10 servings

caribbean sweet potato and bean stew

2 **sweet potatoes (about 1 pound), peeled and cut into 1-inch cubes**

2 **cups frozen cut green beans**

1 **can (about 15 ounces) black beans, rinsed and drained**

1 **can (about 14 ounces) vegetable broth**

1 **onion, sliced**

2 **teaspoons Caribbean jerk seasoning**

½ **teaspoon dried thyme**

¼ **teaspoon salt**

¼ **teaspoon ground cinnamon**

⅓ **cup slivered almonds, toasted***

*To toast almonds, spread in single layer in heavy skillet. Cook over medium heat 1 to 2 minutes or until nuts are lightly browned, stirring frequently.

Combine all ingredients except almonds in **CROCK-POT®** slow cooker. Cover; cook on LOW 5 to 6 hours or until vegetables are tender. Sprinkle with almonds.

Makes 4 servings

all-american meatless sloppy joes

2 cups thinly sliced onions

2 cups chopped green bell peppers

1 can (about 15 ounces) kidney beans, drained and mashed

1 can (8 ounces) tomato sauce

2 tablespoons ketchup

1 tablespoon yellow mustard

2 cloves garlic, finely chopped

1 teaspoon chili powder

1 tablespoon cider vinegar (optional)

4 sandwich rolls

1. Combine all ingredients except vinegar and rolls in **CROCK-POT®** slow cooker. Cover; cook on LOW 5 to 5½ hours or until vegetables are tender.

2. Stir in vinegar, if desired. Serve on rolls.

Makes 4 servings

mediterranean stew

1 medium butternut squash, peeled and cut into 1-inch cubes

2 cups unpeeled eggplant cubes (1 inch)

2 cups sliced zucchini

1 can (about 15 ounces) chickpeas, rinsed and drained

1 package (10 ounces) frozen cut okra

1 cup chopped onion

1 can (8 ounces) tomato sauce

1 medium tomato, chopped

1 medium carrot, sliced

½ cup vegetable broth

⅓ cup raisins

1 clove garlic, minced

½ teaspoon ground cumin

½ teaspoon ground turmeric

¼ teaspoon ground red pepper

¼ teaspoon paprika

¼ teaspoon ground cinnamon

6 to 8 cups hot cooked couscous or rice

Chopped fresh parsley (optional)

Combine all ingredients except couscous and parsley in **CROCK-POT®** slow cooker; mix well. Cover; cook on LOW 8 to 10 hours or until vegetables are crisp-tender. Serve over couscous. Garnish with parsley.

Makes 6 servings

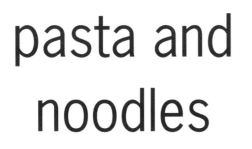

pasta and
noodles

ziti ratatouille

1 large eggplant (about 1½ pounds), peeled and cut into ½-inch cubes

2 zucchini, cut into ½-inch cubes

1 green or red bell pepper, cut into ½-inch pieces

1 onion, chopped

4 cloves garlic, minced

1 jar (24 to 26 ounces) marinara sauce

2 cans (about 14 ounces each) diced tomatoes with garlic and onions

1 package (8 ounces) uncooked ziti pasta

1 can (6 ounces) pitted black olives, drained

Lemon juice and grated Parmesan cheese (optional)

1. Layer eggplant, zucchini, bell pepper, onion, garlic, marinara sauce and tomatoes in **CROCK-POT®** slow cooker. Cover; cook on LOW 4½ hours.

2. Stir in pasta and olives. Cover; cook on LOW 25 minutes or until pasta is tender. Drizzle with lemon juice and sprinkle with cheese, if desired.

Makes 6 to 8 servings

italian hillside garden soup

1 **tablespoon extra virgin olive oil**

1 **cup chopped green bell pepper**

1 **cup chopped onion**

½ **cup sliced celery**

2 **cans (about 14 ounces each) vegetable broth**

1 **can (about 14 ounces) diced tomatoes with basil, garlic and oregano**

1 **can (about 15 ounces) navy beans, rinsed and drained**

1 **medium zucchini, chopped**

1 **cup frozen cut green beans, thawed**

¼ **teaspoon garlic powder**

1 **package (9 ounces) refrigerated cheese-filled tortellini pasta**

3 **tablespoons chopped fresh basil**

Grated Asiago or Parmesan cheese (optional)

1. Heat oil in large skillet over medium-high heat. Add bell pepper, onion and celery; cook and stir 4 minutes or until onion is translucent. Transfer to **CROCK-POT®** slow cooker.

2. Add broth, tomatoes, navy beans, zucchini, green beans, and garlic powder to **CROCK-POT®** slow cooker; mix well. Cover; cook on LOW 7 hours or on HIGH 3½ hours.

3. Turn **CROCK-POT®** slow cooker to HIGH. Add tortellini. Cover; cook on HIGH 20 to 25 minutes or until pasta is tender. Stir in basil. Garnish with cheese.

Makes 6 servings

Tip

Cooking times are guidelines. **CROCK-POT®** slow cookers, just like ovens, cook differently depending on a variety of factors. For example, cooking times will be longer at higher altitudes.

lentil and spinach stew

1 tablespoon olive oil

3 stalks celery, cut into ½-inch pieces

3 carrots, cut into ½-inch pieces

1 medium onion, chopped

3 cloves garlic, minced

4 cups vegetable broth

1 can (about 14 ounces) diced tomatoes

1 cup dried brown lentils, rinsed and sorted

2 teaspoons ground cumin

½ teaspoon salt

½ teaspoon dried basil

¼ teaspoon black pepper

5 cups baby spinach

3 cups hot cooked ditalini pasta

1. Coat inside of **CROCK-POT**® slow cooker with nonstick cooking spray. Heat oil in large skillet over medium-high heat. Add celery, carrots, onion and garlic; cook and stir 3 to 4 minutes or until vegetables begin to soften. Transfer to **CROCK-POT**® slow cooker.

2. Stir broth, tomatoes, lentils, cumin, salt, basil and pepper into **CROCK-POT**® slow cooker. Cover; cook on LOW 8 to 9 hours or until lentils are tender but still hold their shape.

3. Stir in spinach just before serving. Serve over pasta.

Makes 4 servings

homestyle mac and cheese

12 ounces uncooked elbow macaroni (about 3 cups)

2 cans (12 ounces each) evaporated milk

1 cup milk

2 eggs, lightly beaten

⅓ cup all-purpose flour

¼ cup (½ stick) butter, melted

1 teaspoon dry mustard

½ teaspoon salt

¼ teaspoon black pepper

4 cups (16 ounces) shredded sharp Cheddar cheese

Toasted bread crumbs (optional)

1. Coat inside of **CROCK-POT®** slow cooker with nonstick cooking spray. Cook macaroni according to package directions until al dente; drain. Transfer to **CROCK-POT®** slow cooker.

2. Combine evaporated milk, milk, eggs, flour, butter, mustard, salt and pepper in large bowl; mix well. Add to **CROCK-POT®** slow cooker. Stir in cheese until well combined. Cover; cook on LOW 3½ to 4 hours until cheese is melted and macaroni is tender. Stir well; top with toasted bread crumbs, if desired.

Makes 6 to 8 servings

spinach and ricotta stuffed shells

18 uncooked jumbo pasta shells (about half of 12-ounce package)

1 container (15 ounces) ricotta cheese

1 package (10 ounces) frozen chopped spinach, thawed and squeezed dry

½ cup grated Parmesan cheese

1 egg, lightly beaten

1 clove garlic, minced

½ teaspoon salt

1 jar (24 to 26 ounces) marinara sauce

½ cup (2 ounces) shredded mozzarella cheese

1 teaspoon olive oil

1. Cook pasta shells according to package directions until almost tender. Drain well; set aside. Combine ricotta cheese, spinach, Parmesan cheese, egg, garlic and salt in large bowl; mix well.

2. Pour ¼ cup marinara sauce in bottom of **CROCK-POT®** slow cooker. Spoon 2 to 3 tablespoons ricotta mixture into 1 pasta shell and place in bottom of **CROCK-POT®** slow cooker. Repeat with enough additional shells to cover bottom of **CROCK-POT®** slow cooker. Top with ¼ cup marinara sauce. Repeat with remaining pasta shells and filling. Top with remaining marinara sauce and sprinkle with mozzarella cheese. Drizzle with oil. Cover; cook on HIGH 3 to 4 hours or until mozzarella cheese is melted and sauce is hot and bubbly.

Makes 6 servings

garden pasta

1 jar (24 to 26 ounces) spicy tomato basil pasta sauce

2 cups (5 ounces) uncooked bowtie pasta

1 can (about 14 ounces) stewed tomatoes

1 cup small broccoli florets

1 cup finely diced yellow squash or zucchini (or ½ cup of each)

½ cup water

½ cup crumbled feta cheese

¼ cup chopped fresh basil or tarragon

Coat inside of **CROCK-POT®** slow cooker with nonstick cooking spray. Combine pasta sauce, pasta, tomatoes, broccoli, yellow squash and water in **CROCK-POT®** slow cooker; mix well. Cover; cook on LOW 3½ to 4½ hours or on HIGH 2 to 2½ hours or until pasta and vegetables are tender, stirring once halfway through cooking.* Top with cheese and basil.

Stirring once halfway through cooking prevents the pasta on the bottom from becoming overcooked.

Makes 4 to 6 servings

cheese and spinach lasagna

1 container (15 ounces) ricotta cheese

1 package (10 ounces) frozen chopped spinach, thawed and squeezed dry

2 cups (8 ounces) shredded mozzarella cheese, divided

½ cup grated Parmesan cheese, divided

1 egg

1 jar (24 to 26 ounces) pasta sauce

½ cup water

6 uncooked lasagna noodles

1. Coat inside of **CROCK-POT®** slow cooker with nonstick cooking spray. Combine ricotta cheese, spinach, 1½ cups mozzarella cheese, ¼ cup Parmesan cheese and egg in large bowl; mix well.

2. Mix pasta sauce and water in medium bowl. Spoon 1 cup sauce mixture into **CROCK-POT®** slow cooker. Layer 2 noodles over sauce, breaking to fit. Spoon ½ cup sauce mixture over noodles; top with half of ricotta mixture. Add 2 more noodles and remaining ricotta mixture. Top with remaining 2 noodles and remaining pasta sauce.

3. Cover; cook on LOW 4 to 6 hours or until liquid is absorbed and noodles are tender. Turn off heat. Sprinkle with remaining ½ cup mozzarella cheese and ¼ cup Parmesan cheese; let stand, covered, 5 minutes or until cheeses are melted.

Makes 6 servings

no-fuss macaroni and cheese

2 cups (about 8 ounces) uncooked elbow macaroni

4 ounces pasteurized process cheese product, cut into cubes

1 cup (4 ounces) shredded mild Cheddar cheese

½ teaspoon salt

⅛ teaspoon black pepper

1½ cups milk

Combine all ingredients except milk in **CROCK-POT®** slow cooker. Pour in milk. Cover; cook on LOW 2 to 3 hours, stirring after 20 to 30 minutes.

Makes 6 to 8 servings

penne pasta with sun-dried tomatoes and olives

2½ **cups (8 ounces) uncooked penne pasta**

1 **jar (24 to 26 ounces) spicy marinara or tomato basil pasta sauce**

1 **cup water**

½ **cup pitted kalamata olives, halved lengthwise**

⅓ **cup sun-dried tomatoes, packed in oil, drained and chopped**

½ **cup grated Parmesan or Romano cheese**

¼ **cup chopped fresh basil**

Coat inside of **CROCK-POT®** slow cooker with nonstick cooking spray. Combine pasta, marinara sauce, water, olives and sun-dried tomatoes in **CROCK-POT®** slow cooker. Cover; cook on LOW 3½ to 4½ hours or on HIGH 1½ to 2 hours or until pasta is tender, stirring occasionally during cooking.* Stir well; top with cheese and basil.

Stirring pasta during cooking prevents the pasta on the bottom from becoming overcooked.

Makes 4 servings

artichoke pasta

1 tablespoon olive oil

1 cup chopped sweet onion

4 cloves garlic, minced

1 can (28 ounces) crushed tomatoes

1 can (about 14 ounces) artichoke hearts, drained and cut into chunks

1 cup small pimiento-stuffed olives

¾ teaspoon red pepper flakes

8 ounces uncooked fettuccine

½ cup shredded Asiago or Romano cheese

¼ cup chopped fresh basil

1. Coat inside of **CROCK-POT®** slow cooker with nonstick cooking spray. Heat oil in small skillet over medium heat. Add onion; cook and stir 5 minutes or until softened. Add garlic; cook and stir 1 minute. Combine onion mixture, tomatoes, artichokes, olives and red pepper flakes in **CROCK-POT®** slow cooker. Cover; cook on LOW 7 to 8 hours or on HIGH 3 to 4 hours.

2. Cook pasta according to package directions. Drain; top with artichoke sauce, cheese and basil.

Makes 4 servings

vegetable pasta sauce

2 cans (about 14 ounces each) diced
   tomatoes
1 can (about 14 ounces) whole
   tomatoes, undrained
1½ cups sliced mushrooms
1 red bell pepper, diced
1 green bell pepper, diced
1 small yellow squash, cut into ¼-inch
   slices
1 small zucchini, cut into ¼-inch slices
1 can (6 ounces) tomato paste
4 green onions, sliced
2 tablespoons Italian seasoning
1 tablespoon chopped fresh parsley
3 cloves garlic, minced
1 teaspoon salt
1 teaspoon red pepper flakes (optional)
1 teaspoon black pepper
   Hot cooked pasta
   Parmesan cheese and fresh basil
   (optional)

Combine all ingredients except pasta, cheese and basil in **CROCK-POT®** slow cooker; mix well. Cover; cook on LOW 6 to 8 hours. Serve sauce over pasta; top with cheese and basil, if desired.

Makes 4 to 6 servings

portobello bolognese sauce

2 tablespoons extra virgin olive oil

2 cups (6 to 8 ounces) chopped portobello mushrooms

4 cloves garlic, minced

1 jar (24 to 26 ounces) spicy pasta sauce

2 tablespoons tomato paste

1 cup thinly sliced carrots

6 ounces uncooked thin spaghetti

½ cup shredded Parmesan or Romano cheese

¼ cup shredded fresh basil

1. Coat inside of **CROCK-POT®** slow cooker with nonstick cooking spray. Heat oil in large skillet over medium heat. Add mushrooms and garlic; cook and stir 6 minutes or until mushrooms have given up their liquid and liquid has thickened slightly. Transfer to **CROCK-POT®** slow cooker.

2. Add pasta sauce and tomato paste to **CROCK-POT®** slow cooker; mix well. Stir in carrots. Cover; cook on LOW 5 to 6 hours or on HIGH 2½ to 3 hours or until sauce has thickened and carrots are tender.

3. Cook spaghetti according to package directions. Drain; top with sauce, cheese and basil.

Makes 4 servings

three-pepper pasta sauce

1 *each* red, yellow and green bell pepper, cut into 1-inch pieces

2 cans (about 14 ounces each) diced tomatoes

1 cup chopped onion

1 can (6 ounces) tomato paste

2 tablespoons olive oil

4 cloves garlic, minced

1 teaspoon dried basil

1 teaspoon dried oregano

½ teaspoon salt

¼ teaspoon red pepper flakes or black pepper

Hot cooked pasta

Shredded Parmesan or Romano cheese

1. Combine all ingredients except pasta and cheese in **CROCK-POT®** slow cooker. Cover; cook on LOW 7 to 8 hours or until vegetables are tender.

2. Adjust seasonings, if desired. Serve over pasta; top with cheese.

Makes 4 to 6 servings

stuffed manicotti

1 container (15 ounces) ricotta cheese

1½ cups (6 ounces) shredded Italian cheese blend, divided

1 egg

¼ teaspoon ground nutmeg

10 uncooked manicotti shells

2 cans (about 14 ounces each) Italian-seasoned stewed tomatoes

1 cup spicy marinara or tomato basil pasta sauce

Chopped fresh basil or Italian parsley (optional)

1. Coat inside of **CROCK-POT®** slow cooker with nonstick cooking spray. Combine ricotta cheese, 1 cup Italian cheese blend, egg and nutmeg in medium bowl; mix well. Spoon mixture into pastry bag or freezer food storage bag with one corner cut off. Pipe cheese mixture into uncooked manicotti shells.

2. Combine tomatoes and marinara sauce in large bowl. Spoon 1½ cups sauce mixture into **CROCK-POT®** slow cooker. Arrange half of stuffed manicotti in sauce. Repeat layering with 1½ cups sauce, remaining manicotti and remaining sauce. Cover; cook on LOW 2½ to 3 hours or until pasta is tender.

3. Sprinkle remaining ½ cup Italian cheese blend over top. Turn **CROCK-POT®** slow cooker to HIGH. Cover; cook on HIGH 5 minutes or until cheese is melted. Sprinkle with basil, if desired.

Makes 4 servings

slow cooker penne with four cheeses

2½ cups (8 ounces) uncooked penne pasta

3 tablespoons extra virgin olive oil

1 medium onion, chopped

2 cloves garlic, minced

1 teaspoon dried oregano

2 cans (12 ounces each) evaporated milk

2 cups (8 ounces) shredded Gouda cheese

1 cup grated Asiago cheese

1 cup ricotta cheese

½ cup grated Parmesan cheese

2 eggs

¼ teaspoon black pepper

1. Coat inside of **CROCK-POT®** slow cooker with nonstick cooking spray. Bring large pot of water to a boil. Add pasta; cook 3 minutes. Drain pasta and rinse under cold water.

2. Heat oil in large skillet over medium-high heat. Add onion, garlic and oregano; cook and stir 2 to 3 minutes or until onion begins to soften. Transfer to large bowl.

3. Add evaporated milk, cheeses, eggs and pepper to onion mixture; whisk until blended. Add pasta; mix well. Transfer to **CROCK-POT®** slow cooker. Cover; cook on LOW 3½ to 4 hours or until pasta is tender and sauce is set. Serve immediately.

Makes 4 to 6 servings

mediterranean bean soup with orzo and feta

1 **can (about 14 ounces) vegetable broth**

1 **can (about 14 ounces) Italian-style diced tomatoes**

1 **package (10 ounces) frozen mixed vegetables (carrots and peas), thawed**

½ **cup uncooked orzo pasta**

2 **teaspoons dried oregano or basil (or 1 teaspoon each)**

1 **can (about 15 ounces) chickpeas, rinsed and drained**

½ **cup crumbled feta cheese**

1. Coat inside of **CROCK-POT®** slow cooker with nonstick cooking spray. Combine broth, tomatoes, vegetables, pasta and oregano in **CROCK-POT®** slow cooker. Cover; cook on LOW 5 to 6 hours or on HIGH 2 to 3 hours.

2. Stir in chickpeas. Cover; cook on HIGH 10 minutes or until heated through. Ladle into bowls; top with cheese.

Makes 6 servings

6 ingredients
or less

broccoli and cheese strata

2 cups chopped broccoli florets
4 slices (½ inch thick) firm white bread
1 tablespoon butter
1 cup (4 ounces) shredded Cheddar cheese
1½ cups milk
2 eggs plus 2 egg whites
½ teaspoon salt
½ teaspoon hot pepper sauce (optional)
⅛ teaspoon black pepper

1. Lightly coat 1-quart casserole or soufflé dish that fits inside **CROCK-POT®** slow cooker with nonstick cooking spray. Bring large saucepan of water to a boil. Add broccoli; cook 5 minutes or until tender. Drain.

2. Spread one side of each bread slice with butter. Arrange 2 bread slices, buttered sides up, in prepared casserole. Top with cheese, broccoli and remaining 2 bread slices, buttered sides down. Beat milk, eggs, egg whites, salt, hot pepper sauce, if desired, and black pepper in medium bowl. Slowly pour over bread.

3. Place small wire rack in **CROCK-POT®** slow cooker. Pour in 1 cup water. Place casserole on rack. Cover; cook on HIGH 3 hours.

Makes 4 servings

Note
Common ingredients like butter, water, salt and black pepper were not included in the ingredient count.

winter squash and apples

1 teaspoon salt

½ teaspoon black pepper

1 butternut squash (about 2 pounds), peeled and seeded

2 apples, sliced

1 medium onion, quartered and sliced

2 tablespoons butter

1. Combine salt and pepper in small bowl.

2. Cut squash into 2-inch pieces; place in **CROCK-POT®** slow cooker. Add apples and onion. Sprinkle with salt and pepper; stir well. Cover; cook on LOW 6 to 7 hours or until vegetables are tender.

3. Stir in butter and season to taste with additional salt and pepper.

Makes 4 to 6 servings

mile-high enchilada pie

8 corn tortillas (6 inches)

1 jar (12 ounces) salsa

1 can (about 15 ounces) kidney beans, rinsed and drained

1 cup cooked rice

1 cup (4 ounces) shredded pepper jack cheese

Fresh cilantro and sliced red bell pepper (optional)

1. Prepare foil handles by tearing off three 18×3-inch strips heavy foil (or use regular foil folded to double thickness). Crisscross foil strips in spoke design; place in **CROCK-POT®** slow cooker to make lifting tortilla stack easier. Place 1 tortilla on top of foil handles. Top with small amount of salsa, beans, rice and cheese. Continue layering, ending with tortilla and cheese.

2. Cover; cook on LOW 6 to 8 hours or on HIGH 3 to 4 hours. Pull out by foil handles. Garnish with cilantro and bell pepper.

Makes 4 to 6 servings

winter squash
and apples

curried lentils with fruit

5	cups water
1½	cups dried brown lentils, rinsed and sorted
1	Granny Smith apple, peeled and chopped
¼	cup golden raisins
¼	cup plain yogurt
1	teaspoon salt
1	teaspoon curry powder

1. Combine water, lentils, apple and raisins in **CROCK-POT®** slow cooker. Cover; cook on LOW 8 to 9 hours or until lentils are tender. (Lentils should absorb most or all of the water. Slightly tilt **CROCK-POT®** slow cooker to check.)

2. Transfer lentil mixture to large bowl; stir in yogurt, salt and curry powder until blended.

Makes 6 servings

warm salsa and goat cheese dip

1¼ **cups salsa**
 2 **ounces goat cheese crumbles**
 2 **tablespoons coarsely chopped fresh
    cilantro**
    Tortilla chips

1. Bring salsa to a boil in medium saucepan over medium-high heat. Remove from heat and cool slightly.

2. Coat inside of **CROCK-POT® LITTLE DIPPER®** slow cooker with nonstick cooking spray. Fill with heated salsa. Sprinkle with goat cheese and cilantro; do not stir. Serve with tortilla chips.

Makes 1¾ cups

Variation
This dip is also great with pita chips or crisp toasted garlic bread.

pesto rice and beans

1 **can (about 15 ounces) Great Northern beans, rinsed and drained**

1 **can (about 14 ounces) vegetable broth**

¾ **cup uncooked converted long grain rice**

1½ **cups frozen cut green beans, thawed and drained**

½ **cup prepared pesto**
Grated Parmesan cheese (optional)

1. Combine Great Northern beans, broth and rice in **CROCK-POT®** slow cooker. Cover; cook on LOW 2 hours.

2. Stir in green beans. Cover; cook on LOW 1 hour or until rice and beans are tender.

3. Turn off heat. Stir in pesto and cheese, if desired. Let stand, covered, 5 minutes or until cheese is melted. Serve immediately.

Makes 8 servings

chili and cheese "baked" potato supper

4 **russet potatoes (about 2 pounds)**

2 **cups prepared vegetarian chili**

½ **cup (2 ounces) shredded Cheddar cheese**

4 **tablespoons sour cream**

2 **green onions, sliced**

1. Prick potatoes in several places with fork. Wrap potatoes in foil. Place in **CROCK-POT®** slow cooker. Cover; cook on LOW 8 to 10 hours or on HIGH 4 to 5 hours. Carefully unwrap potatoes and place on plates.

2. Heat chili in microwave or on stovetop. Split hot potatoes and top with chili. Top with cheese, sour cream and green onions.

Makes 4 servings

apricot and brie dip

½ cup dried apricots, finely chopped

⅓ cup plus 1 tablespoon apricot preserves, divided

¼ cup apple juice

1 round wheel Brie cheese (2 pounds), rind removed, cut into cubes

Crackers or bread slices

Combine apricots, ⅓ cup apricot preserves and apple juice in **CROCK-POT®** slow cooker. Cover; cook on HIGH 40 minutes. Stir in cheese. Cover; cook on HIGH 30 to 40 minutes or until cheese is melted. Stir in remaining 1 tablespoon preserves. Turn **CROCK-POT®** slow cooker to LOW; serve warm with crackers.

Makes 3 cups

cheesy ranch potatoes

3 **pounds unpeeled red potatoes, quartered**

1 **cup water**

½ **cup prepared ranch dressing**

½ **cup grated Parmesan or shredded Cheddar cheese**

¼ **cup minced fresh chives**

1. Place potatoes in **CROCK-POT®** slow cooker. Add water. Cover; cook on LOW 7 to 9 hours or on HIGH 4 to 6 hours or until potatoes are tender.

2. Stir in ranch dressing, cheese and chives. Break up potatoes into chunks with spoon.

Makes 8 servings

braised beets with cranberries

2½ **pounds medium beets, peeled and cut into wedges**

1 **cup cranberry juice**

½ **cup sweetened dried cranberries**

2 **tablespoons quick-cooking tapioca**

2 **tablespoons butter, cubed**

2 **tablespoons honey**

½ **teaspoon salt**

⅓ **cup crumbled blue cheese (optional)**
   Thinly sliced or grated orange peel (optional)

1. Combine beets, cranberry juice, cranberries, tapioca, butter, honey and salt in **CROCK-POT®** slow cooker. Cover; cook on LOW 7 to 8 hours or until beets are tender.

2. Transfer beets to serving bowl with slotted spoon. Pour half of cooking liquid over beets. Serve warm, at room temperature or chilled. Sprinkle with cheese and orange peel, if desired.

Makes 6 to 8 servings

artichoke and nacho cheese dip

2 cans (10¾ ounces each) condensed nacho cheese soup, undiluted

1 can (14 ounces) quartered artichoke hearts, drained and coarsely chopped

1 can (5 ounces) evaporated milk

1 cup (4 ounces) shredded pepper jack cheese

2 tablespoons chopped fresh chives, divided

½ teaspoon paprika

Crackers or chips

1. Combine soup, artichokes, evaporated milk, cheese, 1 tablespoon chives and paprika in **CROCK-POT®** slow cooker. Cover; cook on LOW 2 hours.

2. Stir well; sprinkle with remaining 1 tablespoon chives. Serve with crackers.

Makes about 4 cups

chili con queso

1 package (16 ounces) pasteurized process cheese product, cubed

1 can (10 ounces) diced tomatoes with green chiles

1 cup sliced green onions

2 teaspoons ground coriander

2 teaspoons ground cumin

¾ teaspoon hot pepper sauce

Green onion strips (optional)

Sliced jalapeño pepper (optional)*

Tortilla chips

*Jalapeño peppers can sting and irritate the skin, so wear rubber gloves when handling peppers and do not touch your eyes.

1. Combine cheese product, tomatoes, sliced green onions, coriander and cumin in **CROCK-POT®** slow cooker; mix well. Cover; cook on LOW 2 to 3 hours or until heated through.*

2. Garnish with green onion strips and jalapeño pepper. Serve with tortilla chips.
*Dip will be very hot; use caution when serving.

Makes 3 cups

Serving Suggestion
Cut pita bread into triangles and toast in a preheated 400°F oven for 5 minutes or until crisp.

cheesy corn and peppers

2 pounds frozen corn

2 poblano peppers, chopped *or* 1 green bell pepper and 1 jalapeño pepper, seeded and finely chopped*

2 tablespoons butter, cubed

1 teaspoon salt

½ teaspoon ground cumin

¼ teaspoon black pepper

1 cup (4 ounces) shredded sharp Cheddar cheese

3 ounces cream cheese, cubed

Poblano and jalapeño peppers can sting and irritate the skin, so wear rubber gloves when handling peppers and do not touch your eyes.

1. Coat inside of **CROCK-POT®** slow cooker with nonstick cooking spray. Combine corn, poblano peppers, butter, salt, cumin and black pepper in **CROCK-POT®** slow cooker. Cover; cook on HIGH 2 hours.

2. Stir in cheeses. Cover; cook on HIGH 15 minutes or until cheeses are melted.

Makes 8 servings

slow cooker cheese soup

2 cans (10¾ ounces each) condensed cream of celery soup, undiluted

4 cups (16 ounces) shredded Cheddar cheese

1 teaspoon paprika, plus additional for garnish

1 teaspoon vegetarian Worcestershire sauce

1¼ cups half-and-half

Salt and black pepper

Chopped fresh chives (optional)

1. Combine soup, cheese, 1 teaspoon paprika and Worcestershire sauce in **CROCK-POT®** slow cooker. Cover; cook on LOW 2 to 3 hours.

2. Add half-and-half; stir until blended. Cover; cook on LOW 20 minutes. Season to taste with salt and pepper. Sprinkle with additional paprika and chives, if desired.

Makes 4 servings

Tip

Turn simple soup into a super supper by serving it in individual bread bowls. Cut a small slice from the tops of small round loaves of a hearty bread (such as Italian or sourdough) and remove the insides, leaving a 1½-inch shell. Pour in soup and serve.

southwestern mac and cheese

1 **package (8 ounces) uncooked elbow macaroni**

1 **can (about 14 ounces) diced tomatoes with green peppers and onions**

1 **can (10 ounces) diced tomatoes with green chiles**

1½ **cups salsa**

3 **cups (12 ounces) shredded Mexican cheese blend, divided**

1. Coat inside of **CROCK-POT®** slow cooker with nonstick cooking spray. Layer macaroni, tomatoes, salsa and 2 cups cheese in **CROCK-POT®** slow cooker. Cover; cook on LOW 3 to 4 hours or until macaroni is tender.

2. Sprinkle remaining 1 cup cheese over macaroni. Cover; cook on LOW 15 minutes or until cheese is melted.

Makes 6 servings

soups and
chilies

spring pea and mint soup

4 **carrots, cut into ¼-inch slices, divided**

3 **stalks celery, cut into ¼-inch slices, divided**

8 **cups water**

2 **medium onions, coarsely chopped**

3 **leeks, coarsely chopped**

1 **bunch fresh mint**

1 **package (32 ounces) frozen peas** *or* **4 cups fresh spring peas**

1 **tablespoon fresh lemon juice**

Kosher salt and black pepper

Crème fraîche or sour cream

1. Reserve 1 cup carrot slices and 1 cup celery slices; set aside. Combine water, remaining carrots and celery, onions, leeks and mint in **CROCK-POT®** slow cooker. Cover; cook on HIGH 5 hours.

2. Strain broth and return to **CROCK-POT®** slow cooker; discard solids. Add peas, lemon juice and reserved carrots and celery. Cover; cook on LOW 4 to 5 hours or on HIGH 2 to 3 hours.

3. Season with salt and pepper. Serve with crème fraîche.

Makes 6 to 8 servings

tomato soup with ditalini

2 tablespoons extra virgin olive oil

2 carrots, chopped (about 1 cup)

½ medium bulb fennel, chopped
(about 1 cup)

1 medium onion, chopped (about 1 cup)

3 cloves garlic, minced

2 cans (28 ounces each) whole plum
tomatoes

4 cups vegetable broth

3 tablespoons tomato paste

1 teaspoon dried basil

1 teaspoon salt

¼ teaspoon black pepper

3 cups hot cooked ditalini pasta
Grated Parmesan cheese

1. Coat inside of **CROCK-POT®** slow cooker with nonstick cooking spray. Add oil, carrots, fennel, onion, garlic, tomatoes, broth, tomato paste, basil, salt and pepper. Cover; cook on LOW 7 to 8 hours or on HIGH 3 to 4 hours or until vegetables are very tender.

2. Working in batches, transfer soup to blender; blend until smooth. Return blended soup to **CROCK-POT®** slow cooker. Serve soup over pasta; sprinkle with cheese.

Makes 6 to 8 servings

vegetarian chili

1 tablespoon vegetable oil

1 cup chopped onion

1 cup chopped red bell pepper

2 tablespoons minced jalapeño pepper*

1 clove garlic, minced

1 can (28 ounces) crushed tomatoes

1 can (about 15 ounces) black beans, rinsed and drained

1 can (about 15 ounces) chickpeas, rinsed and drained

½ cup corn

¼ cup tomato paste

1 teaspoon sugar

1 teaspoon ground cumin

1 teaspoon dried basil

1 teaspoon chili powder

¼ teaspoon black pepper

Sour cream and shredded Cheddar cheese (optional)

*Jalapeño peppers can sting and irritate the skin, so wear rubber gloves when handling peppers and do not touch your eyes.

1. Heat oil in large skillet over medium-high heat. Add onion, bell pepper, jalapeño pepper and garlic; cook and stir 5 minutes or until tender. Transfer to **CROCK-POT®** slow cooker.

2. Add tomatoes, beans, chickpeas, corn, tomato paste, sugar, cumin, basil, chili powder and black pepper to **CROCK-POT®** slow cooker; mix well. Cover; cook on LOW 4 to 5 hours. Serve with sour cream and cheese, if desired.

Makes 4 servings

creamy cauliflower bisque

1 **pound frozen cauliflower florets**

1 **pound baking potatoes, cut into 1-inch cubes**

1 **cup chopped onion**

2 **cans (about 14 ounces each) vegetable broth**

½ **teaspoon dried thyme**

¼ **teaspoon garlic powder**

⅛ **teaspoon ground red pepper**

1 **cup evaporated milk**

2 **tablespoons butter**

½ **teaspoon salt**

¼ **teaspoon black pepper**

1 **cup (4 ounces) shredded sharp Cheddar cheese**

¼ **cup finely chopped fresh parsley**

¼ **cup finely chopped green onions**

1. Combine cauliflower, potatoes, onion, broth, thyme, garlic powder and ground red pepper in **CROCK-POT®** slow cooker. Cover; cook on LOW 8 hours or on HIGH 4 hours.

2. Working in batches, transfer soup to blender; blend until smooth. Return blended soup to **CROCK-POT®** slow cooker. Stir in evaporated milk, butter, salt and black pepper until blended.

3. Serve with cheese, parsley and green onions.

Makes 9 servings

corn and two bean chili

1 can (about 15 ounces) pinto or kidney beans, rinsed and drained

1 can (about 15 ounces) black beans, rinsed and drained

1 can (about 14 ounces) fire-roasted diced tomatoes

1 cup salsa

1 cup frozen corn, thawed

½ cup minced onion

1 teaspoon chili powder

1 teaspoon ground cumin

½ cup sour cream

1 cup (4 ounces) shredded Cheddar cheese

1. Coat inside of **CROCK-POT®** slow cooker with nonstick cooking spray. Combine beans, tomatoes, salsa, corn, onion, chili powder and cumin in **CROCK-POT®** slow cooker; mix well. Cover; cook on LOW 5 to 6 hours or on HIGH 2½ to 3 hours or until bubbly.

2. Serve with sour cream and cheese.

Makes 4 servings

pesto, white bean and pasta stew

1 **can (28 ounces) Italian-seasoned diced tomatoes**

2 **cups vegetable broth**

1 **green bell pepper, cut into pieces**

1 **cup uncooked elbow macaroni or ditalini pasta**

1 **can (about 15 ounces) cannellini or Great Northern beans, rinsed and drained**

¼ **cup prepared pesto**

⅓ **cup grated Parmesan or Romano cheese**

1. Coat inside of **CROCK-POT**® slow cooker with nonstick cooking spray. Combine tomatoes, broth, bell pepper and pasta in **CROCK-POT**® slow cooker. Cover; cook on LOW 4 to 5 hours or on HIGH 2 to 2½ hours or until bell pepper and pasta are tender.

2. Stir in beans and pesto. Cover; cook on HIGH 10 to 15 minutes or until heated through. Serve with cheese.

Makes 6 servings

roasted tomato-basil soup

2 cans (28 ounces each) whole tomatoes, drained and 3 cups liquid reserved

2½ tablespoons packed dark brown sugar

1 medium onion, finely chopped

3 cups vegetable broth

3 tablespoons tomato paste

¼ teaspoon ground allspice

1 can (5 ounces) evaporated milk

¼ cup shredded fresh basil (about 10 large leaves)

Salt and black pepper

1. Preheat oven to 450°F. Line baking sheet with foil; spray with nonstick cooking spray. Arrange tomatoes on foil in single layer. Sprinkle with brown sugar; top with onion. Bake 25 minutes or until tomatoes look dry and light brown. Let cool slightly; finely chop.

2. Place tomato mixture, 3 cups reserved liquid from tomatoes, broth, tomato paste and allspice in **CROCK-POT®** slow cooker; mix well. Cover; cook on LOW 8 hours or on HIGH 4 hours.

3. Stir in evaporated milk and basil; season with salt and pepper. Cover; cook on HIGH 30 minutes or until heated through.

Makes 6 servings

slow cooker veggie stew

1	tablespoon vegetable oil
⅔	cup carrot slices
½	cup diced onion
2	cloves garlic, chopped
2	cans (about 14 ounces each) vegetable broth
1½	cups chopped green cabbage
½	cup cut green beans
½	cup diced zucchini
1	tablespoon tomato paste
½	teaspoon dried basil
½	teaspoon dried oregano
¼	teaspoon salt

1. Heat oil in medium skillet over medium-high heat. Add carrot, onion and garlic; cook and stir 5 minutes or until tender. Transfer to **CROCK-POT®** slow cooker.

2. Add broth, cabbage, green beans, zucchini, tomato paste, basil, oregano and salt to **CROCK-POT®** slow cooker; mix well. Cover; cook on LOW 8 to 10 hours or on HIGH 4 to 5 hours.

Makes 4 to 6 servings

tortilla soup

2 cans (about 14 ounces each) vegetable broth

1 can (about 14 ounces) diced tomatoes with jalapeño peppers

2 cups chopped carrots

2 cups frozen corn, thawed

1½ cups chopped onions

1 can (8 ounces) tomato sauce

1 tablespoon chili powder

1 teaspoon ground cumin

¼ teaspoon garlic powder

Shredded Monterey Jack cheese

Crushed tortilla chips

1. Combine broth, tomatoes, carrots, corn, onions, tomato sauce, chili powder, cumin and garlic powder in **CROCK-POT®** slow cooker. Cover; cook on LOW 6 to 8 hours.

2. Ladle soup into bowls; top with cheese and tortilla chips.

Makes 6 servings

butternut squash, chickpea and lentil stew

2 cups peeled and diced butternut squash (½-inch pieces)

2 cups vegetable broth

1 can (about 15 ounces) chickpeas, rinsed and drained

1 can (about 14 ounces) fire-roasted diced tomatoes

1 cup chopped sweet onion

¾ cup dried brown lentils, rinsed and sorted

2 teaspoons ground cumin or coriander (or 1 teaspoon each)

¾ teaspoon salt

Olive oil (optional)

Fresh thyme (optional)

Coat inside of **CROCK-POT®** slow cooker with nonstick cooking spray. Combine squash, broth, chickpeas, tomatoes, onion, lentils, cumin and salt in **CROCK-POT®** slow cooker. Cover; cook on LOW 8 to 9 hours or on HIGH 4 to 4½ hours or until squash and lentils are tender. Ladle into shallow bowls. Drizzle with oil, if desired; garnish with thyme.

Makes 6 servings

curried sweet potato and carrot soup

2 large sweet potatoes, peeled and cut into ¾-inch cubes (about 5 cups)

2 cups baby carrots

1 small onion, chopped

¾ teaspoon curry powder

½ teaspoon salt

½ teaspoon black pepper

½ teaspoon ground cinnamon

¼ teaspoon ground ginger

4 cups vegetable broth

¾ cup half-and-half

1 tablespoon maple syrup

Candied ginger (optional)

1. Combine sweet potatoes, carrots, onion, curry powder, salt, pepper, cinnamon and ground ginger in **CROCK-POT®** slow cooker. Add broth; mix well. Cover; cook on LOW 7 to 8 hours.

2. Working in batches, transfer soup to blender; blend until smooth. Return blended soup to **CROCK-POT®** slow cooker. (Or use immersion blender.) Stir in half-and-half and maple syrup. Turn **CROCK-POT®** slow cooker to HIGH. Cover; cook on HIGH 15 minutes to reheat. Garnish with candied ginger.

Makes 8 servings

potato cheddar soup

2 **pounds unpeeled new red potatoes, cut into ½-inch cubes**

¾ **cup coarsely chopped carrots**

1 **medium onion, coarsely chopped**

½ **teaspoon salt**

3 **cups vegetable broth**

1 **cup half-and-half**

¼ **teaspoon black pepper**

2 **cups (8 ounces) shredded Cheddar cheese**

1. Place potatoes, carrots, onion and salt in **CROCK-POT®** slow cooker. Pour in broth. Cover; cook on LOW 6 to 7 hours or on HIGH 3 to 3½ hours or until vegetables are tender.

2. Stir in half-and-half and pepper. Cover; cook on HIGH 15 minutes. Turn off heat. Let stand, uncovered, 5 minutes. Stir in cheese until melted.

Makes 6 servings

Serving Suggestion
Try this soup topped with whole wheat croutons.

mediterranean chili

2 cans (about 28 ounces each) chickpeas, rinsed and drained

1 can (28 ounces) diced tomatoes

1 can (about 14 ounces) vegetable broth

2 onions, chopped

10 kalamata olives, chopped

4 cloves garlic, minced

2 teaspoons ground cumin

1/4 teaspoon ground red pepper

1/2 cup chopped fresh mint

1 teaspoon chopped fresh oregano

1/2 teaspoon grated lemon peel

1 cup crumbled feta cheese

1. Combine chickpeas, tomatoes, broth, onions, olives, garlic, cumin and ground red pepper in **CROCK-POT®** slow cooker; mix well. Cover; cook on LOW 7 to 8 hours or on HIGH 3½ hours.

2. Stir in mint, oregano and lemon peel; top with cheese.

Makes 6 servings

french onion soup

6 tablespoons (¾ stick) butter

3 pounds yellow onions, sliced

1 tablespoon sugar

2 to 3 tablespoons dry white wine or water

8 cups vegetable broth

8 to 16 slices French bread

½ cup (2 ounces) shredded Gruyère or Swiss cheese

1. Melt butter in large skillet over medium-low heat. Add onions; cover and cook 10 minutes or until onions are tender and transparent but not browned.

2. Sprinkle sugar over onions; cook and stir 8 to 10 minutes or until onions are caramelized. Transfer onions to **CROCK-POT**® slow cooker. Add wine to skillet; bring to a boil, scraping up any browned bits. Add to **CROCK-POT**® slow cooker. Stir in broth. Cover; cook on LOW 8 hours or on HIGH 6 hours.

3. Preheat broiler. To serve, ladle soup into individual broilerproof bowls. Top each with 1 or 2 bread slices and about 1 tablespoon cheese. Broil until cheese is melted and bubbly.

Makes 8 servings

Variation
Substitute 1 cup dry white wine for 1 cup of vegetable broth.

black bean soup with lime

2 cans (about 15 ounces each) black beans, undrained

1 can (about 14 ounces) vegetable broth

1½ cups chopped onions

1½ teaspoons chili powder

¾ teaspoon ground cumin

¼ teaspoon garlic powder

⅛ to ¼ teaspoon red pepper flakes

1 medium lime, cut into wedges

½ cup sour cream

2 tablespoons extra virgin olive oil

2 tablespoons chopped fresh cilantro

1. Coat inside of **CROCK-POT**® slow cooker with nonstick cooking spray. Add beans, broth, onions, chili powder, cumin, garlic powder and red pepper flakes. Cover; cook on LOW 7 hours or on HIGH 3½ hours or until onions are very soft.

2. Process 1 cup soup mixture in blender until smooth; return to **CROCK-POT**® slow cooker. Repeat with additional soup until desired consistency is reached. Let stand 15 to 20 minutes before serving.

3. Ladle soup into bowls; squeeze lime wedge over each serving. Top with sour cream, oil and cilantro.

Makes 4 servings

Tip
Brighten the flavor of dishes cooked in the **CROCK-POT**® slow cooker by adding fresh herbs or fresh lemon or lime juice before serving.

curried eggplant, squash and chickpea stew

1 tablespoon plus 1 teaspoon olive oil

2 cups diced red bell peppers

1 cup diced onion

1 tablespoon plus 2 teaspoons curry powder

4 cloves garlic, minced

2 teaspoons salt

5 cups cubed peeled eggplant

3 cups cubed peeled acorn or butternut squash

2⅔ cups rinsed and drained canned chickpeas

2 cups vegetable broth or water

¾ cup dry white wine

Hot pepper sauce (optional)

1 cup plain yogurt (optional)

½ cup chopped fresh parsley (optional)

1. Heat oil in large skillet over medium heat. Add bell peppers and onion; cook and stir 5 minutes or until softened. Stir in curry powder, garlic and salt; cook and stir 1 minute. Transfer to **CROCK-POT**® slow cooker.

2. Add eggplant, squash, chickpeas, broth and wine; mix well. Cover; cook on LOW 8 to 10 hours or until vegetables are tender.

3. Season to taste with hot pepper sauce, if desired. Garnish with yogurt and parsley.

Makes 8 servings

hearty white bean minestrone

5 cups vegetable broth

2 cans (about 15 ounces each) cannellini beans, rinsed and drained

1 can (about 14 ounces) diced tomatoes

2 russet potatoes (about 1 pound), peeled and cut into ½-inch cubes

1 medium onion, chopped

3 carrots, chopped

3 stalks celery, chopped

3 cloves garlic, minced

6 cups chopped fresh kale

Grated Parmesan cheese (optional)

1. Combine broth, beans, tomatoes, potatoes, onion, carrots, celery and garlic in **CROCK-POT®** slow cooker; mix well. Cover; cook on LOW 7 hours.

2. Turn **CROCK-POT®** slow cooker to HIGH. Stir in kale. Cover; cook on HIGH 1 to 2 hours or until vegetables are tender. Garnish with cheese.

Makes 6 servings

hearty vegetable and potato chowder

2 cups vegetable broth

1 can (10¾ ounces) condensed cream of mushroom soup, undiluted

1 package (10 ounces) frozen mixed vegetables (corn, carrots, peas and green beans)

2 medium russet potatoes (about 1 pound), cut into ½-inch cubes

2 to 3 teaspoons minced garlic

1½ teaspoons dried thyme

½ cup (2 ounces) shredded Colby-Jack or Cheddar cheese (optional)

½ teaspoon black pepper (optional)

1. Coat inside of **CROCK-POT®** slow cooker with nonstick cooking spray. Combine broth, soup, vegetables, potatoes, garlic and thyme in **CROCK-POT®** slow cooker; mix well. Cover; cook on LOW 7 to 8 hours on HIGH 3 to 4 hours.

2. Stir well; garnish with cheese and black pepper.

Makes 6 servings

vegetable and red lentil soup

- 1 **can (about 14 ounces) vegetable broth**
- 1 **can (about 14 ounces) diced tomatoes**
- 2 **medium zucchini or yellow summer squash, chopped**
- 1 **red or yellow bell pepper, chopped**
- ½ **cup thinly sliced carrots**
- ½ **cup dried red lentils, rinsed and sorted**
- ½ **teaspoon salt**
- ½ **teaspoon sugar**
- ¼ **teaspoon black pepper**
- 2 **tablespoons chopped fresh basil or thyme**
- ½ **cup croutons or shredded cheese**

1. Combine broth, tomatoes, zucchini, bell pepper, carrots, lentils, salt, sugar and black pepper in **CROCK-POT®** slow cooker; mix well. Cover; cook on LOW 8 hours or on HIGH 4 hours or until lentils and vegetables are tender.

2. Serve with basil and croutons.

Makes 6 servings

Tip

When adapting your favorite recipe for a **CROCK-POT®** slow cooker, reduce the liquid by as much as half, because foods don't lose as much moisture during slow cooking as during conventional cooking.

peppery potato soup

2 cans (about 14 ounces each) vegetable broth

4 small unpeeled baking potatoes, halved and sliced crosswise

1 large onion, quartered and sliced

1 stalk celery, sliced

½ teaspoon salt

½ teaspoon black pepper

1 cup half-and-half

¼ cup all-purpose flour

1 tablespoon butter

Fresh parsley (optional)

1. Combine broth, potatoes, onion, celery, salt and pepper in **CROCK-POT®** slow cooker; mix well. Cover; cook on LOW 6 to 7 hours.

2. Stir half-and-half into flour in medium bowl until smooth; stir mixture into **CROCK-POT®** slow cooker. Cover; cook on LOW 1 hour.

3. Slightly mash soup with potato masher. Cook, uncovered, on LOW 30 minutes or until slightly thickened. Stir in butter just before serving. Garnish with parsley.

Makes 6 servings

wisconsin beer and cheese soup

3 slices pumpernickel or rye bread, cut into ½-inch cubes

1 can (about 14 ounces) vegetable broth

1 cup beer

¼ cup finely chopped onion

2 cloves garlic, minced

¾ teaspoon dried thyme

1½ cups (6 ounces) shredded American cheese

1½ cups (6 ounces) shredded sharp Cheddar cheese

1 cup milk

½ teaspoon paprika

1. Preheat oven to 425°F. Place bread on baking sheet in single layer. Bake 10 to 12 minutes or until crisp, stirring once. Set aside.

2. Combine broth, beer, onion, garlic and thyme in **CROCK-POT®** slow cooker; mix well. Cover; cook on LOW 4 hours.

3. Turn **CROCK-POT®** slow cooker to HIGH. Stir in cheeses, milk and paprika. Cover; cook on HIGH 45 minutes to 1 hour or until soup is hot and cheeses are melted. Stir well; serve with croutons.

Makes 4 servings

Tip
Choose a light-tasting beer when making this soup.

chipotle vegetable chili with chocolate

2 tablespoons olive oil

1 onion, chopped

1 green bell pepper, chopped

1 red bell pepper, chopped

1 cup frozen corn

1 can (28 ounces) diced tomatoes

1 can (about 15 ounces) black beans, rinsed and drained

1 can (about 15 ounces) pinto beans, rinsed and drained

1 tablespoon chili powder

1 teaspoon ground cumin

½ teaspoon ground chipotle pepper

1 ounce semisweet chocolate, chopped

Sour cream and shredded Cheddar cheese (optional)

1. Heat oil in large nonstick skillet over medium-high heat. Add onion and bell peppers; cook and stir 4 minutes or until softened. Stir in corn; cook 3 minutes. Transfer to **CROCK-POT®** slow cooker.

2. Stir tomatoes, beans, chili powder, cumin and chipotle pepper into **CROCK-POT®** slow cooker. Cover; cook on LOW 6 to 7 hours or until vegetables are tender. Stir chocolate into **CROCK-POT®** slow cooker until melted. Garnish with sour cream and cheese.

Makes 6 servings

potato and spinach soup with gouda

9 **medium Yukon Gold potatoes, peeled and cubed (about 6 cups)**

2 **cans (about 14 ounces each) vegetable broth**

1 **small red onion, finely chopped**

5 **ounces baby spinach**

½ **cup water**

½ **teaspoon salt**

¼ **teaspoon ground red pepper**

¼ **teaspoon black pepper**

2½ **cups (10 ounces) shredded smoked Gouda cheese, divided**

1 **can (12 ounces) evaporated milk**

1 **tablespoon olive oil**

4 **cloves garlic, thinly sliced**

Chopped fresh parsley

1. Combine potatoes, broth, onion, spinach, water, salt, ground red pepper and black pepper in **CROCK-POT®** slow cooker. Cover; cook on LOW 10 hours or until potatoes are tender.

2. Slightly mash potatoes in **CROCK-POT®** slow cooker; stir in 2 cups cheese and evaporated milk. Turn **CROCK-POT®** slow cooker to HIGH. Cover; cook on HIGH 15 to 20 minutes or until cheese is melted.

3. Meanwhile, heat oil in small skillet over low heat. Add garlic; cook and stir until golden brown. Ladle soup into bowls. Top with remaining cheese, garlic and parsley.

Makes 8 to 10 servings

sensational
side dishes

cheesy mashed potato casserole

- **4** **pounds Yukon Gold potatoes, cut into 1-inch pieces**
- **2** **cups vegetable broth**
- **3** **tablespoons butter, cubed**
- **½** **cup milk, heated**
- **⅓** **cup sour cream**
- **½** **teaspoon salt**
- **¼** **teaspoon black pepper**
- **2** **cups (8 ounces) shredded sharp Cheddar cheese, plus additional for garnish**

1. Coat inside of **CROCK-POT®** slow cooker with nonstick cooking spray. Add potatoes and broth; dot with butter. Cover; cook on LOW 4½ to 5 hours or until potatoes are very tender.

2. Mash potatoes with potato masher; stir in milk, sour cream, salt and pepper. Stir in cheese until melted. Serve immediately or hold on WARM setting 2 to 3 hours. Garnish with additional cheese.

Makes 10 to 12 servings

southwestern corn and beans

1 tablespoon olive oil

1 large onion, diced

1 to 2 jalapeño peppers, diced*

1 clove garlic, minced

2 cans (about 15 ounces each) light red kidney beans, rinsed and drained

1 bag (16 ounces) frozen corn, thawed

1 can (about 14 ounces) diced tomatoes

1 green bell pepper, cut into 1-inch pieces

2 teaspoons chili powder

¾ teaspoon salt

½ teaspoon ground cumin

½ teaspoon black pepper

Sour cream or plain yogurt (optional)

Sliced black olives (optional)

*Jalapeño peppers can sting and irritate the skin, so wear rubber gloves when handling peppers and do not touch your eyes.

1. Heat oil in medium skillet over medium heat. Add onion, jalapeño pepper and garlic; cook and stir 5 minutes or until softened. Transfer to **CROCK-POT®** slow cooker.

2. Add beans, corn, tomatoes, bell pepper, chili powder, salt, cumin and black pepper; mix well. Cover; cook on LOW 7 to 8 hours or on HIGH 2 to 3 hours. Serve with sour cream and olives, if desired.

Makes 6 servings

Tip

For a party, spoon this colorful dish into hollowed-out bell peppers or bread bowls.

french carrot medley

2 cups sliced carrots

¾ cup orange juice

1 can (4 ounces) sliced mushrooms, undrained

4 stalks celery, sliced

2 tablespoons chopped onion

½ teaspoon dried dill weed

Salt and black pepper

¼ cup water

2 teaspoons cornstarch

1. Combine carrots, orange juice, mushrooms, celery, onion, dill, salt and pepper in **CROCK-POT®** slow cooker; mix well. Cover; cook on LOW 3 to 4 hours or on HIGH 2 hours.

2. Stir water into cornstarch in small bowl until smooth. Stir into **CROCK-POT®** slow cooker. Cover; cook on HIGH 15 minutes or until thickened.

Makes 6 servings

mashed rutabagas and potatoes

2 pounds rutabagas, peeled and cut into ½-inch pieces

1 pound potatoes, peeled and cut into ½-inch pieces

½ cup milk, warmed

½ teaspoon ground nutmeg

2 tablespoons chopped fresh parsley

1. Place rutabagas and potatoes in **CROCK-POT®** slow cooker; add enough water to cover vegetables. Cover; cook on LOW 6 hours or on HIGH 3 hours or until rutabagas and potatoes are tender.

2. Transfer vegetables to large bowl with slotted spoon. Discard cooking liquid. Mash vegetables with potato masher or electric mixer. Add milk and nutmeg; stir until smooth. Stir in parsley before serving.

Makes 8 servings

french carrot medley

swiss cheese scalloped potatoes

2 pounds baking potatoes, thinly sliced
½ cup finely chopped onion
¼ teaspoon salt
¼ teaspoon ground nutmeg
2 tablespoons butter, cubed
½ cup milk
2 tablespoons all-purpose flour
¾ cup (3 ounces) shredded Swiss cheese
¼ cup finely chopped green onions (optional)

1. Layer half of potatoes, ¼ cup onion, ⅛ teaspoon salt, ⅛ teaspoon nutmeg and 1 tablespoon butter in **CROCK-POT®** slow cooker. Repeat layers. Cover; cook on LOW 7 hours or on HIGH 4 hours.

2. Remove potatoes to serving dish with slotted spoon; keep warm.

3. Whisk milk into flour in small bowl until smooth; stir into cooking liquid. Stir in cheese. Turn **CROCK-POT®** slow cooker to HIGH. Cover; cook on HIGH 10 minutes or until slightly thickened. Stir; pour cheese mixture over potatoes. Sprinkle with green onions, if desired.

Makes 5 to 6 servings

spring vegetable ragoût

1 tablespoon olive oil

2 leeks, thinly sliced

3 cloves garlic, minced

3 cups small cherry tomatoes, halved

1⅔ cups frozen corn

8 ounces yellow squash, halved lengthwise and cut into ½-inch pieces (about 1¼ cups)

1 cup vegetable broth

½ cup frozen shelled edamame

1 package (4 ounces) shredded carrots

1 teaspoon dried tarragon

1 teaspoon dried basil

1 teaspoon dried oregano

Salt and black pepper

Minced fresh parsley (optional)

1. Heat oil in large skillet over medium heat. Add leeks and garlic; cook and stir just until fragrant. Transfer to **CROCK-POT®** slow cooker.

2. Add tomatoes, corn, squash, broth, edamame, carrots, tarragon, basil and oregano; mix well. Cover; cook on LOW 6 to 8 hours or on HIGH 3 to 4 hours or until vegetables are tender. Season to taste with salt and pepper. Garnish with parsley.

Makes 6 servings

braised sweet and sour cabbage and apples

2 tablespoons butter

6 cups coarsely shredded red cabbage

1 large sweet apple, peeled and cut into bite-size pieces

½ cup raisins

½ cup apple cider

3 tablespoons cider vinegar, divided

2 tablespoons packed dark brown sugar

½ teaspoon salt

¼ teaspoon black pepper

3 whole cloves

1. Melt butter in large skillet or saucepan over medium heat. Add cabbage; cook and stir 3 minutes or until cabbage is glossy. Transfer to **CROCK-POT®** slow cooker.

2. Add apple, raisins, apple cider, 2 tablespoons vinegar, brown sugar, salt, pepper and cloves; mix well. Cover; cook on LOW 2½ to 3 hours.

3. Remove cloves and stir in remaining 1 tablespoon vinegar before serving.

Makes 4 to 6 servings

lemon dill parsnips and turnips

2 cups vegetable broth

¼ cup chopped green onions

¼ cup lemon juice

1 tablespoon dried dill weed

1 teaspoon minced garlic

4 turnips, peeled and cut into ½-inch pieces

3 parsnips, peeled and cut into ½-inch pieces

¼ cup cold water

1 tablespoon cornstarch

1. Combine broth, green onions, lemon juice, dill and garlic in **CROCK-POT**® slow cooker. Add turnips and parsnips; mix well. Cover; cook on LOW 3 to 4 hours or on HIGH 1 to 3 hours.

2. Turn **CROCK-POT**® slow cooker to HIGH. Stir water into cornstarch in small bowl until smooth. Stir into **CROCK-POT**® slow cooker. Cover; cook on HIGH 15 minutes or until thickened.

Makes 10 servings

blue cheese potatoes

2 pounds red potatoes, peeled and cut into ½-inch pieces
1¼ cups chopped green onions, divided
2 tablespoons olive oil, divided
1 teaspoon dried basil
½ teaspoon salt
¼ teaspoon black pepper
½ cup crumbled blue cheese

1. Layer potatoes, 1 cup green onions, 1 tablespoon oil, basil, salt and pepper in **CROCK-POT**® slow cooker. Cover; cook on LOW 7 hours or on HIGH 4 hours.

2. Gently stir in cheese and remaining 1 tablespoon oil. Turn **CROCK-POT**® slow cooker to HIGH. Cover; cook on HIGH 5 minutes to allow flavors to blend. Sprinkle with remaining ¼ cup green onions.

Makes 5 servings

asian kale and chickpeas

1 tablespoon sesame oil
1 medium onion, thinly sliced
2 jalapeño peppers, chopped*
2 cloves garlic, minced
2 teaspoons grated fresh ginger
8 cups chopped kale
1 cup vegetable broth
2 cans (about 15 ounces each) chickpeas, rinsed and drained
1 teaspoon grated lime peel
1 tablespoon fresh lime juice
2 cups hot cooked rice

Jalapeño peppers can sting and irritate the skin, so wear rubber gloves when handling peppers and do not touch your eyes.

1. Coat inside of **CROCK-POT**® slow cooker with nonstick cooking spray. Heat oil in large nonstick skillet over medium-high heat. Add onion, jalapeño peppers, garlic and ginger; cook and stir 1 minute. Add kale; cook and stir 2 minutes or until slightly wilted. Transfer mixture to **CROCK-POT**® slow cooker.

2. Add broth and chickpeas; mix well. Cover; cook on LOW 3 hours or until kale is tender.

3. Turn off heat. Stir in lime peel and juice. Serve over rice.

Makes 4 servings

blue cheese potatoes

cheesy cauliflower

3 **pounds cauliflower florets**

¼ **cup water**

5 **tablespoons butter**

1 **cup finely chopped onion**

6 **tablespoons all-purpose flour**

¼ **teaspoon dry mustard**

2 **cups milk**

2 **cups (8 ounces) shredded sharp Cheddar cheese**

½ **teaspoon salt**

¼ **teaspoon black pepper**

1. Coat inside of **CROCK-POT**® slow cooker with nonstick cooking spray. Add cauliflower and water.

2. Melt butter in medium saucepan over medium-high heat. Add onion; cook and stir 4 to 5 minutes or until slightly softened. Stir in flour and mustard until well blended. Cook 3 minutes, stirring constantly. Whisk in milk until smooth. Bring to a boil; cook 1 to 2 minutes or until thickened. Stir in cheese, salt and pepper; stir until cheese is melted.

3. Pour cheese mixture over cauliflower in **CROCK-POT**® slow cooker. Cover; cook on LOW 4 to 4½ hours or until cauliflower is tender.

Makes 8 to 10 servings

mediterranean red potatoes

**3 unpeeled medium red potatoes,
cut into bite-size pieces**

⅔ cup fresh or frozen pearl onions

1 tablespoon olive oil

1 clove garlic, minced

¾ teaspoon dried Italian seasoning

¼ teaspoon black pepper

1 small tomato, seeded and chopped

2 ounces feta cheese, crumbled

2 tablespoons chopped black olives

1. Combine potatoes, onions, oil, garlic, Italian seasoning and pepper in 1½-quart soufflé dish that will fit in **CROCK-POT®** slow cooker; toss to coat. Cover dish tightly with foil.

2. Make foil handles using three 18×3-inch strips of heavy-duty foil or use regular foil folded to double thickness. Crisscross foil in spoke design; place across bottom and up side of stoneware. Place soufflé dish in center of strips in **CROCK-POT®** slow cooker. Pull foil strips up and over dish.

3. Pour hot water into **CROCK-POT®** slow cooker to about 1½ inches from top of soufflé dish. Cover; cook on LOW 7 to 8 hours.

4. Use foil handles to lift dish out of **CROCK-POT®** slow cooker. Stir tomato, cheese and olives into potato mixture.

Makes 4 servings

jim's mexican-style spinach

3 packages (10 ounces each) frozen chopped spinach

1 tablespoon canola oil

1 onion, chopped

1 clove garlic, minced

2 Anaheim chiles, roasted, peeled and minced*

3 fresh tomatillos, roasted, husks removed and chopped**

Sour cream (optional)

*To roast chiles, heat heavy skillet over medium-high heat. Add chiles; cook until blackened all over, turning occasionally with tongs. Place chiles in brown paper bag for 2 to 5 minutes. Scrape off charred skin. Cut off top and remove core. Slice chiles lengthwise; scrape off veins and any remaining seeds with sharp knife.

**To roast tomatillos, heat heavy skillet over medium heat. Add tomatillos; cook until husks are brown and interior flesh is soft, turning often. Remove and discard husks when cool enough to handle.

1. Place frozen spinach in **CROCK-POT®** slow cooker.

2. Heat oil in large skillet over medium heat. Add onion and garlic; cook and stir 5 minutes or until onion is soft but not browned. Add chiles and tomatillos; cook and stir 3 to 4 minutes. Add mixture to **CROCK-POT®** slow cooker. Cover; cook on LOW 4 to 6 hours. Stir before serving. Serve with sour cream, if desired.

Makes 6 servings

buttery vegetable gratin

- **3 leeks, halved lengthwise and cut into 1-inch pieces**
- **1 red bell pepper, cut into ½-inch pieces**
- **5 tablespoons butter, divided**
- **¼ cup grated Parmesan cheese**
- **1 teaspoon chopped fresh thyme**
- **¾ teaspoon salt**
- **⅜ teaspoon black pepper**
- **2 zucchini (about 1½ pounds total), cut into ¾-inch-thick slices**
- **2 yellow squash (about 1½ pounds total), cut into ¾-inch-thick slices**
- **1½ cups fresh bread crumbs**

1. Generously coat inside of **CROCK-POT®** slow cooker with nonstick cooking spray. Combine leeks and bell pepper in **CROCK-POT®** slow cooker. Dot with 1 tablespoon butter. Sprinkle with 1 tablespoon cheese, ½ teaspoon thyme, ¼ teaspoon salt and ⅛ teaspoon black pepper.

2. Add zucchini in single layer, overlapping as necessary. Dot with 1 tablespoon butter. Sprinkle with 1 tablespoon cheese, remaining ½ teaspoon thyme, ¼ teaspoon salt and ⅛ teaspoon black pepper.

3. Arrange yellow squash in single layer over zucchini, overlapping as necessary. Dot with 1 tablespoon butter. Sprinkle with remaining 2 tablespoons cheese, ¼ teaspoon salt and ⅛ teaspoon black pepper. Cover; cook on LOW 4 to 5 hours or until vegetables are soft.

4. Melt remaining 2 tablespoons butter in large skillet over medium-high heat. Add bread crumbs; cook and stir 6 minutes or until crisp and golden brown. Cool slightly. Sprinkle over vegetable gratin just before serving.

Makes 12 servings

apple and carrot casserole

6 **carrots, cut into ½-inch slices**

4 **apples, peeled and sliced**

¼ **cup plus 1 tablespoon all-purpose flour**

1 **tablespoon packed brown sugar**

½ **teaspoon ground nutmeg**

1 **tablespoon butter, cubed**

½ **cup orange juice**

½ **teaspoon salt**

Layer carrots and apples in **CROCK-POT®** slow cooker. Combine flour, brown sugar and nutmeg in small bowl; sprinkle over carrots and apples. Dot with butter; pour in juice. Sprinkle with salt. Cover; cook on LOW 3½ to 4 hours or until carrots are crisp-tender.

Makes 6 servings

polenta-style corn casserole

1   **can (about 14 ounces) vegetable broth**
½   **cup cornmeal**
1   **can (about 8 ounces) corn, drained**
1   **can (4 ounces) diced mild green chiles, drained**
¼   **cup diced red bell pepper**
½   **teaspoon salt**
¼   **teaspoon black pepper**
1   **cup (4 ounces) shredded Cheddar cheese**

1. Pour broth into **CROCK-POT®** slow cooker. Whisk in cornmeal. Add corn, chiles, bell pepper, salt and black pepper. Cover; cook on LOW 4 to 5 hours or on HIGH 2 to 3 hours.

2. Stir in cheese. Cook, uncovered, on LOW 15 to 30 minutes or until cheese melts.

Makes 6 servings

Serving Suggestion
For firmer polenta, divide cooked corn mixture among lightly greased individual ramekins or spread in pie plate. Cover and refrigerate until firm. Serve cold or at room temperature.

red hot applesauce

10 to 12 apples, peeled and chopped
¾ cup hot cinnamon candies
½ cup apple juice or water

Combine apples, candies and apple juice in **CROCK-POT®** slow cooker. Cover; cook on LOW 7 to 8 hours or on HIGH 4 hours or until desired consistency. Serve warm or chilled.

Makes 6 servings

scalloped tomatoes and corn

1 **can (about 15 ounces) cream-style corn**

1 **can (about 14 ounces) diced tomatoes**

¾ **cup saltine or soda cracker crumbs**

1 **egg, lightly beaten**

2 **teaspoons sugar**

¾ **teaspoon black pepper**

Chopped fresh tomatoes (optional)

Chopped fresh parsley (optional)

Combine corn, diced tomatoes, cracker crumbs, egg, sugar and pepper in **CROCK-POT®** slow cooker; mix well. Cover; cook on LOW 4 to 6 hours. Sprinkle with fresh tomatoes and parsley before serving, if desired.

Makes 4 to 6 servings

fennel braised with tomato

1 tablespoon olive oil

2 bulbs fennel, trimmed and cut into wedges

1 onion, sliced

1 clove garlic, sliced

4 tomatoes, chopped

⅔ cup vegetable broth or water

3 tablespoons dry white wine or vegetable broth

1 tablespoon chopped fresh marjoram *or* 1 teaspoon dried marjoram

¼ teaspoon salt

¼ teaspoon black pepper

1. Heat oil in large skillet over medium heat. Add fennel, onion and garlic; cook and stir 5 minutes or until onion is soft and translucent. Transfer to **CROCK-POT®** slow cooker.

2. Add tomatoes, broth, wine, marjoram, salt and pepper; mix well. Cover; cook on LOW 2 to 3 hours or on HIGH 1 to 1½ hours or until vegetables are tender, stirring occasionally.

Makes 6 servings

scalloped corn

4 cups frozen corn, thawed, divided
2 tablespoons butter
½ cup chopped onion
3 tablespoons all-purpose flour
1 cup milk
½ teaspoon salt
½ teaspoon dried thyme
¼ teaspoon black pepper
⅛ teaspoon ground nutmeg
Fresh thyme (optional)

1. Process 2 cups corn in food processor until coarsely chopped. Transfer to **CROCK-POT®** slow cooker; stir in remaining 2 cups corn.

2. Melt butter in small saucepan over medium heat. Add onion; cook and stir 5 minutes or until tender. Add flour; cook 1 minute, stirring constantly. Whisk in milk; bring to a boil. Boil 1 minute or until thickened, whisking constantly. Stir in salt, dried thyme, pepper and nutmeg. Pour over corn in **CROCK-POT®** slow cooker; mix well. Cover; cook on LOW 3½ to 4 hours or until mixture is bubbly around edge. Garnish with fresh thyme.

Makes 6 servings

garden potato casserole

1¼ **pounds unpeeled baking potatoes,
thinly sliced**

 1 **green or red bell pepper, thinly sliced**

¼ **cup finely chopped onion**

 2 **tablespoons butter, cubed, divided**

½ **teaspoon salt**

½ **teaspoon dried thyme**

 Black pepper

 1 **yellow squash, thinly sliced**

 1 **cup (4 ounces) shredded sharp
Cheddar cheese**

 Chopped fresh chives

1. Place potatoes, bell pepper, onion, 1 tablespoon butter, salt, thyme and black pepper in **CROCK-POT®** slow cooker; mix well. Layer squash evenly over potato mixture; dot with remaining 1 tablespoon butter. Cover; cook on LOW 7 hours or on HIGH 4 hours.

2. Remove casserole to serving bowl. Sprinkle with cheese; let stand 2 to 3 minutes or until cheese melts. Sprinkle with chives.

Makes 5 servings

coconut-lime sweet potatoes with walnuts

2½ **pounds sweet potatoes, peeled and cut into 1-inch pieces**

8 **ounces shredded carrots**

¾ **cup flaked coconut, divided**

3 **tablespoons sugar**

1 **tablespoon butter, melted**

½ **teaspoon salt**

⅓ **cup walnuts, toasted and coarsely chopped, divided***

2 **teaspoons grated lime peel**

*To toast walnuts, spread in single layer in heavy skillet. Cook over medium heat 1 to 2 minutes or until nuts are lightly browned, stirring frequently.

1. Combine sweet potatoes, carrots, ½ cup coconut, sugar, butter and salt in **CROCK-POT®** slow cooker. Cover; cook on LOW 5 to 6 hours or until sweet potatoes are tender.

2. Heat small skillet over medium heat. Add remaining ¼ cup coconut; cook and stir 4 minutes or until lightly browned. Transfer to small bowl; cool completely.

3. Mash sweet potatoes. Stir in 3 tablespoons walnuts and lime peel. Sprinkle with remaining walnuts and toasted coconut.

Makes 8 servings

cheesy broccoli casserole

2 packages (10 ounces each) frozen chopped broccoli, thawed

1 can (10¾ ounces) condensed cream of celery soup, undiluted

1¼ cups (5 ounces) shredded sharp Cheddar cheese, divided

¼ cup finely chopped onion

1 teaspoon paprika

1 teaspoon hot pepper sauce

½ teaspoon celery seed

1 cup crushed potato chips or saltine crackers

1. Coat inside of **CROCK-POT®** slow cooker with nonstick cooking spray. Combine broccoli, soup, 1 cup cheese, onion, paprika, hot pepper sauce and celery seed in **CROCK-POT®** slow cooker; mix well. Cover; cook on LOW 5 to 6 hours or on HIGH 2½ to 3 hours.

2. Sprinkle with potato chips and remaining ¼ cup cheese. Cook, uncovered, on LOW 30 to 60 minutes or on HIGH 15 to 30 minutes or until cheese melts.

Makes 4 to 6 servings

Variation

Substitute thawed chopped spinach for the broccoli and top with crushed crackers or spicy croutons.

grain-packed
plates

wild rice and dried cherry risotto

1 cup salted dry-roasted peanuts
2 tablespoons dark sesame oil, divided
1 cup chopped onion
6 ounces uncooked wild rice
1 cup diced carrots
1 cup chopped green or red bell pepper
½ cup dried cherries
⅛ to ¼ teaspoon red pepper flakes
4 cups hot water
¼ cup teriyaki or soy sauce
1 teaspoon salt

1. Coat inside of **CROCK-POT**® slow cooker with nonstick cooking spray. Heat large skillet over medium-high heat. Add peanuts; cook and stir 2 to 3 minutes or until peanuts begin to brown. Transfer peanuts to plate; set aside.

2. Heat 2 teaspoons oil in same skillet over medium-high heat. Add onion; cook and stir 6 minutes or until browned. Transfer to **CROCK-POT**® slow cooker.

3. Add wild rice, carrots, bell pepper, cherries, red pepper flakes and water; mix well. Cover; cook on HIGH 3 hours.

4. Turn off heat. Let stand, uncovered, 15 minutes until liquid is absorbed. Stir in teriyaki sauce, peanuts, remaining oil and salt.

Makes 8 to 10 servings

wild rice and mushroom casserole

2 tablespoons olive oil

½ medium red onion, finely diced

1 green bell pepper, finely diced

8 ounces white mushrooms, thinly sliced

1 can (about 14 ounces) diced tomatoes

2 cloves garlic, minced

1 teaspoon dried oregano

1 teaspoon paprika

2 tablespoons butter

2 tablespoons all-purpose flour

1½ cups milk

2 cups (8 ounces) shredded pepper jack, Cheddar or Swiss cheese

1 teaspoon salt

½ teaspoon black pepper

2 cups wild rice, cooked according to package directions

1. Coat inside of **CROCK-POT®** slow cooker with nonstick cooking spray. Heat oil in large skillet over medium heat. Add onion, bell pepper and mushrooms; cook and stir 5 to 6 minutes or until vegetables soften. Add tomatoes, garlic, oregano and paprika; cook and stir until heated through. Remove to large bowl.

2. Melt butter in same skillet over medium heat; whisk in flour. Cook and stir 4 to 5 minutes or until smooth and golden. Whisk in milk; bring to a boil. Whisk in cheese until blended and smooth. Stir in salt and black pepper.

3. Add wild rice to vegetables. Fold in cheese sauce; mix gently. Transfer to **CROCK-POT®** slow cooker. Cover; cook on LOW 4 to 6 hours or on HIGH 2 to 3 hours.

Makes 4 to 6 servings

layered mexican-style casserole

2 **cans (about 15 ounces each) hominy, drained***

1 **can (about 15 ounces) black beans, rinsed and drained**

1 **can (about 14 ounces) diced tomatoes with garlic, basil and oregano**

1 **cup thick and chunky salsa**

1 **can (6 ounces) tomato paste**

½ **teaspoon ground cumin**

3 **flour tortillas (9 inches)**

2 **cups (8 ounces) shredded Monterey Jack cheese**

¼ **cup sliced black olives**

*Hominy is corn that has been treated to remove the germ and hull. It can be found with the canned vegetables or beans in most supermarkets.

1. Prepare foil handles (see Note). Coat inside of **CROCK-POT®** slow cooker with nonstick cooking spray.

2. Combine hominy, beans, tomatoes, salsa, tomato paste and cumin in large bowl; mix well.

3. Press 1 tortilla into bottom of **CROCK-POT®** slow cooker. (Edges of tortilla may turn up slightly.) Top with one third of hominy mixture and one third of cheese. Repeat layers. Press remaining tortilla on top and top with remaining hominy mixture. Reserve remaining cheese.

4. Cover; cook on LOW 6 to 8 hours or on HIGH 2 to 3 hours. Turn off heat. Sprinkle with remaining cheese and olives; let stand, covered, 5 minutes. Pull out tortilla stack with foil handles.

Makes 6 servings

Note

To make foil handles, tear off three 18×3-inch strips of heavy-duty foil or use regular foil folded to double thickness. Crisscross foil strips in spoke design and place in **CROCK-POT®** slow cooker to make lifting of tortilla stack easier.

quinoa and vegetable medley

2 medium sweet potatoes, cut into ½-inch-thick slices

1 medium eggplant, peeled and cut into ½-inch cubes

1 green bell pepper, sliced

1 tomato, cut into wedges

1 small onion, cut into wedges

½ teaspoon salt

¼ teaspoon ground red pepper

¼ teaspoon black pepper

1 cup uncooked quinoa

2 cups vegetable broth or water

2 cloves garlic, minced

½ teaspoon dried thyme

¼ teaspoon dried marjoram

1. Coat inside of **CROCK-POT®** slow cooker with nonstick cooking spray. Combine sweet potatoes, eggplant, bell pepper, tomato, onion, salt, ground red pepper and black pepper in **CROCK-POT®** slow cooker; mix well.

2. Place quinoa in fine-mesh strainer; rinse well. Add quinoa to vegetable mixture in **CROCK-POT®** slow cooker. Stir in broth, garlic, thyme and marjoram. Cover; cook on LOW 5 hours or on HIGH 2½ hours or until quinoa is tender and broth is absorbed.

Makes 6 servings

mexican hot pot

1 tablespoon canola oil

1 medium onion, chopped

3 cloves garlic, minced

2 teaspoons red pepper flakes

2 teaspoons dried oregano

1 teaspoon ground cumin

1 can (28 ounces) whole tomatoes, drained and chopped

2 cups corn

1 can (about 15 ounces) chickpeas, rinsed and drained

1 can (about 15 ounces) pinto beans, rinsed and drained

1 cup water

Shredded lettuce

1. Heat oil in large skillet over medium-high heat. Add onion and garlic; cook and stir 5 minutes. Add red pepper flakes, oregano and cumin; mix well. Transfer to **CROCK-POT®** slow cooker.

2. Add tomatoes, corn, chickpeas, beans and water; mix well. Cover; cook on LOW 7 to 8 hours or on HIGH 2 to 3 hours. Serve with shredded lettuce.

Makes 6 servings

garlic and herb polenta

3 **tablespoons butter, divided**

8 **cups water**

2 **cups yellow cornmeal**

2 **teaspoons minced garlic**

2 **teaspoons salt**

3 **tablespoons chopped fresh herbs such as parsley, chives, thyme or chervil (or a combination)**

Grease inside of **CROCK-POT®** slow cooker with 1 tablespoon butter. Add water, cornmeal, garlic, salt and remaining 2 tablespoons butter; mix well. Cover; cook on LOW 4 hours or on HIGH 3 hours, stirring occasionally. Stir in chopped herbs just before serving.

Makes 6 servings

Tip

Polenta may also be poured into a greased pan and allowed to cool until set. Cut into squares or slices to serve. For even more great flavor, chill polenta slices until firm, then grill or fry until golden brown.

lentil stew over couscous

3 cups dried lentils (1 pound), rinsed and sorted

3 cups water

1 can (about 14 ounces) vegetable broth

1 can (about 14 ounces) diced tomatoes

1 large onion, chopped

1 green bell pepper, chopped

4 stalks celery, chopped

1 carrot, halved lengthwise and sliced

2 cloves garlic, chopped

1 teaspoon dried marjoram

¼ teaspoon black pepper

1 tablespoon olive oil

1 tablespoon cider vinegar

4½ to 5 cups hot cooked couscous

1. Combine lentils, water, broth, tomatoes, onion, bell pepper, celery, carrot, garlic, marjoram and black pepper in **CROCK-POT®** slow cooker; mix well. Cover; cook on LOW 8 to 9 hours or until vegetables are tender.

2. Stir in oil and vinegar. Serve over couscous.

Makes 12 servings

Tip

Lentil stew keeps well in the refrigerator for up to 1 week. The stew can also be frozen in an airtight container for up to 3 months.

barley with currants and pine nuts

1 **tablespoon butter**
1 **small onion, finely chopped**
2 **cups vegetable broth**
½ **cup uncooked pearl barley**
⅓ **cup currants**
½ **teaspoon salt**
¼ **teaspoon black pepper**
¼ **cup pine nuts**

1. Melt butter in small skillet over medium-high heat. Add onion; cook and stir about 5 minutes or lightly browned. Transfer to **CROCK-POT®** slow cooker. Add broth, barley, currants, salt and pepper; mix well. Cover; cook on LOW 3 hours.

2. Stir in pine nuts; serve immediately.

Makes 4 servings

polenta lasagna

4 cups boiling water

1½ cups whole grain yellow cornmeal

4 teaspoons finely chopped fresh marjoram

1 tablespoon olive oil

1 pound mushrooms, sliced

1 cup chopped leeks

1 clove garlic, minced

½ cup (2 ounces) shredded mozzarella cheese

2 tablespoons chopped fresh basil

1 tablespoon chopped fresh oregano

⅛ teaspoon black pepper

2 medium red bell peppers, chopped

¼ cup water

¼ cup grated Parmesan cheese

1. Coat inside of **CROCK-POT®** slow cooker with nonstick cooking spray. Combine 4 cups boiling water and cornmeal in **CROCK-POT®** slow cooker; mix well. Stir in marjoram. Cover; cook on LOW 3 to 4 hours or on HIGH 1 to 2 hours, stirring occasionally. Cover and chill about 1 hour or until firm.

2. Heat oil in medium nonstick skillet over medium heat. Add mushrooms, leeks and garlic; cook and stir 5 minutes or until leeks are crisp-tender. Stir in mozzarella cheese, basil, oregano and black pepper.

3. Place bell peppers and water in food processor or blender; process until smooth.

4. Cut cold polenta in half and place one half in bottom of **CROCK-POT®** slow cooker. Top with half of bell pepper mixture, half of mushroom mixture and 2 tablespoons Parmesan cheese. Place remaining polenta over Parmesan cheese; layer with remaining bell pepper and mushroom mixtures and Parmesan cheese. Cover; cook on LOW 3 hours or until cheese is melted and polenta is golden brown.

Makes 6 servings

vegetarian sausage rice

2 cups chopped green bell peppers

1 can (about 15 ounces) dark kidney beans, rinsed and drained

1 can (about 14 ounces) diced tomatoes with bell peppers and onions

1 cup chopped onion

1 cup sliced celery

1 cup water, divided

¾ cup uncooked converted long grain rice

1¼ teaspoons salt

1 teaspoon hot pepper sauce

½ teaspoon dried thyme

½ teaspoon red pepper flakes

3 whole bay leaves

1 package (8 ounces) frozen meatless breakfast patties, thawed

2 tablespoons extra virgin olive oil

½ cup chopped fresh parsley

1. Combine bell peppers, beans, tomatoes, onion, celery, ½ cup water, rice, salt, hot pepper sauce, thyme, red pepper flakes and bay leaves in **CROCK-POT®** slow cooker; mix well. Cover; cook on LOW 4 to 5 hours. Remove and discard bay leaves.

2. Dice meatless patties. Heat oil in large nonstick skillet over medium-high heat. Add patties; cook and stir 2 minutes or until lightly browned. Transfer to **CROCK-POT®** slow cooker. Do not stir.

3. Add remaining ½ cup water to skillet. Bring to a boil over high heat; cook 1 minute, scraping up browned bits on bottom of skillet. Add liquid and parsley to **CROCK-POT®** slow cooker; stir gently to blend.

Makes 8 cups

mushroom barley stew

- **1 tablespoon olive oil**
- **1 medium onion, finely chopped**
- **1 cup chopped carrots (about 2 carrots)**
- **1 clove garlic, minced**
- **1 cup uncooked pearl barley**
- **1 cup dried wild mushrooms, broken into pieces**
- **1 teaspoon salt**
- **½ teaspoon dried thyme**
- **½ teaspoon black pepper**
- **5 cups vegetable broth**

1. Heat oil in medium skillet over medium-high heat. Add onion, carrots and garlic; cook and stir 5 minutes or until tender. Transfer to **CROCK-POT®** slow cooker.

2. Add barley, mushrooms, salt, thyme and pepper. Stir in broth; mix well. Cover; cook on LOW 6 to 7 hours.

Makes 4 to 6 servings

Tip
To turn this thick, robust stew into a soup, add 2 to 3 additional cups of broth. Cook the same length of time.

red beans and rice

2 cans (about 15 ounces each) red beans, undrained

1 can (about 14 ounces) diced tomatoes

½ cup chopped celery

½ cup chopped green bell pepper

½ cup chopped green onions

2 cloves garlic, minced

1 to 2 teaspoons hot pepper sauce

1 teaspoon vegetarian Worcestershire sauce

1 whole bay leaf

3 cups hot cooked rice

1. Combine beans, tomatoes, celery, bell pepper, green onions, garlic, hot pepper sauce, Worcestershire sauce and bay leaf in **CROCK-POT®** slow cooker; mix well. Cover; cook on LOW 4 to 6 hours or on HIGH 2 to 3 hours.

2. Mash bean mixture slightly in **CROCK-POT®** slow cooker with potato masher until mixture thickens. Cover; cook on HIGH 30 minutes to 1 hour. Remove and discard bay leaf. Serve bean mixture over rice.

Makes 6 servings

italian eggplant with millet and pepper stuffing

¼ **cup uncooked millet**

2 **small eggplants (about ¾ pound total)**

¼ **cup chopped red bell pepper, divided**

¼ **cup chopped green bell pepper, divided**

1 **teaspoon olive oil**

1 **clove garlic, minced**

1½ **cups vegetable broth**

½ **teaspoon ground cumin**

½ **teaspoon dried oregano**

⅛ **teaspoon red pepper flakes**

1. Cook and stir millet in large heavy skillet over medium heat 5 minutes or until golden. Transfer to small bowl; set aside.

2. Cut eggplants lengthwise into halves. Scoop out flesh, leaving ¼-inch-thick shell. Reserve shells; chop eggplant flesh. Combine 1 tablespoon red bell pepper and 1 tablespoon green bell pepper in small bowl; set aside.

3. Heat oil in same skillet over medium heat. Add chopped eggplant, remaining red and green bell pepper and garlic; cook and stir about 8 minutes or until eggplant is tender. Transfer to **CROCK-POT®** slow cooker. Add millet, broth, cumin, oregano and red pepper flakes; mix well. Cover; cook on LOW 4½ hours or until all liquid is absorbed and millet is tender.

4. Fill eggplant shells with millet mixture. Sprinkle with reserved bell peppers. Carefully place filled shells in **CROCK-POT®** slow cooker. Turn **CROCK-POT®** slow cooker to HIGH. Cover; cook on HIGH 1½ to 2 hours.

Makes 4 servings

mushroom risotto

3	tablespoons extra virgin olive oil
8	ounces sliced mushrooms
½	cup chopped shallots
½	cup chopped onion
3	cloves garlic, minced
1½	cups uncooked arborio rice
½	cup Madeira wine
4½	cups vegetable broth
½	cup grated Romano cheese
3	tablespoons butter
3	tablespoons chopped fresh parsley
¼	teaspoon black pepper

1. Heat oil in large skillet over medium-high heat. Add mushrooms; cook and stir 6 to 7 minutes or until mushrooms begin to brown. Stir in shallots, onion and garlic; cook and stir 2 to 3 minutes or until vegetables begin to soften. Add rice; cook and stir 1 minute. Add wine; cook and stir 1 minute or until almost absorbed.

2. Transfer mixture to **CROCK-POT®** slow cooker. Add broth; mix well. Cover; cook on HIGH 2 hours or until liquid is absorbed and rice is tender.

3. Turn off heat; stir in cheese, butter, parsley and pepper.

Makes 4 servings

mexican corn bread pudding

1 **can (about 14 ounces) cream-style corn**

¾ **cup yellow cornmeal**

1 **can (4 ounces) diced mild green chiles**

2 **eggs**

2 **tablespoons sugar**

2 **tablespoons vegetable oil**

2 **teaspoons baking powder**

¾ **teaspoon salt**

½ **cup (2 ounces) shredded Cheddar cheese**

Coat inside of 2-quart **CROCK-POT**® slow cooker with nonstick cooking spray. Combine corn, cornmeal, chiles, eggs, sugar, oil, baking powder and salt in medium bowl; mix well. Pour into **CROCK-POT**® slow cooker. Cover; cook on LOW 2 to 2½ hours or until center is set. Turn off heat. Sprinkle cheese over top. Cover; let stand 5 minutes or until cheese is melted.

Makes 8 servings

creamy barley risotto

3 cups vegetable broth
1 cup uncooked pearl barley
1 large leek, thinly sliced and separated into rings
1 cup frozen baby peas, thawed
1 tablespoon lemon juice
½ to 1 teaspoon grated lemon peel
2 tablespoons butter, cut into 4 pieces
  Salt and black pepper
  Shaved Parmesan cheese
  Chopped fresh parsley (optional)

1. Coat inside of **CROCK-POT®** slow cooker with nonstick cooking sprasy. Combine broth, barley and leek in **CROCK-POT®** slow cooker; mix well. Cover; cook on LOW 4 to 5 hours or on HIGH 2 to 2½ hours or until most of liquid is absorbed.

2. Stir in peas, lemon juice and lemon peel. Turn **CROCK-POT®** slow cooker to HIGH. Cover; cook on HIGH 10 minutes or until heated through. Stir in butter until melted. Season to taste with salt and pepper. Top with cheese and parsley, if desired.

Makes 4 servings

greek rice

2 tablespoons butter

1¾ cups uncooked converted long grain rice

2 cans (about 14 ounces each) vegetable broth

1 teaspoon Greek seasoning

1 teaspoon dried oregano

1 cup pitted kalamata olives, drained and chopped

¾ cup chopped roasted red peppers

Crumbled feta cheese

Chopped fresh Italian parsley (optional)

1. Melt butter in large nonstick skillet over medium-high heat. Add rice; cook and stir 4 minutes or until golden brown. Transfer to **CROCK-POT®** slow cooker. Stir in broth, Greek seasoning and oregano; mix well. Cover; cook on LOW 4 hours or until liquid is absorbed and rice is tender.

2. Stir in olives and roasted red peppers. Cover; cook on LOW 5 minutes. Top with cheese; garnish with parsley.

Makes 6 to 8 servings

barley salad

2 onions, chopped

2 sweet potatoes, diced

1 cup uncooked pearl barley

1 teaspoon salt

½ teaspoon ground cinnamon

¼ teaspoon ground red pepper (optional)

1½ cups water

2 apples, peeled and chopped

1 cup dried cranberries

1 cup chopped pecans

1. Spread onions and sweet potatoes in bottom of **CROCK-POT**® slow cooker. Add barley, salt, cinnamon and ground red pepper, if desired. Pour in water. Cover; cook on LOW 4 hours or on HIGH 2 hours.

2. Stir in apples, cranberries and pecans. Serve warm or at room temperature.

Makes 16 servings

recipe index

recipe index

metric conversion chart

VOLUME MEASUREMENTS (dry)

1/8 teaspoon = 0.5 mL
1/4 teaspoon = 1 mL
1/2 teaspoon = 2 mL
3/4 teaspoon = 4 mL
1 teaspoon = 5 mL
1 tablespoon = 15 mL
2 tablespoons = 30 mL
1/4 cup = 60 mL
1/3 cup = 75 mL
1/2 cup = 125 mL
2/3 cup = 150 mL
3/4 cup = 175 mL
1 cup = 250 mL
2 cups = 1 pint = 500 mL
3 cups = 750 mL
4 cups = 1 quart = 1 L

VOLUME MEASUREMENTS (fluid)

1 fluid ounce (2 tablespoons) = 30 mL
4 fluid ounces (1/2 cup) = 125 mL
8 fluid ounces (1 cup) = 250 mL
12 fluid ounces (1 1/2 cups) = 375 mL
16 fluid ounces (2 cups) = 500 mL

WEIGHTS (mass)

1/2 ounce = 15 g
1 ounce = 30 g
3 ounces = 90 g
4 ounces = 120 g
8 ounces = 225 g
10 ounces = 285 g
12 ounces = 360 g
16 ounces = 1 pound = 450 g

DIMENSIONS

1/16 inch = 2 mm
1/8 inch = 3 mm
1/4 inch = 6 mm
1/2 inch = 1.5 cm
3/4 inch = 2 cm
1 inch = 2.5 cm

OVEN TEMPERATURES

250°F = 120°C
275°F = 140°C
300°F = 150°C
325°F = 160°C
350°F = 180°C
375°F = 190°C
400°F = 200°C
425°F = 220°C
450°F = 230°C

BAKING PAN AND DISH EQUIVALENTS

Utensil	Size in Inches	Size in Centimeters	Volume	Metric Volume
Baking or Cake Pan (square or rectangular)	8×8×2	20×20×5	8 cups	2 L
	9×9×2	23×23×5	10 cups	2.5 L
	13×9×2	33×23×5	12 cups	3 L
Loaf Pan	8½×4½×2½	21×11×6	6 cups	1.5 L
	9×9×3	23×13×7	8 cups	2 L
Round Layer Cake Pan	8×1½	20×4	4 cups	1 L
	9×1½	23×4	5 cups	1.25 L
Pie Plate	8×1½	20×4	4 cups	1 L
	9×1½	23×4	5 cups	1.25 L
Baking Dish or Casserole			1 quart/4 cups	1 L
			1½ quart/6 cups	1.5 L
			2 quart/8 cups	2 L
			3 quart/12 cups	3 L